MW00907123

MICROSOFT
WORD 5.5

PC
VERSION

Microsoft
P R E S S
®

PETER RINEARSON

PUBLISHED BY
Microsoft Press
A Division of Microsoft Corporation
One Microsoft Way
Redmond, Washington 98052-6399

Library of Congress Cataloging-in-Publication Data

Rinearson, Peter, 1954-
   Microsoft Word 5.5 / Peter Rinearson.
      p.   cm. -- (Microsoft quick reference)
   ISBN 1-55615-352-X
   1. Microsoft Word (Computer program) 2. Word processing--Computer
programs.   I. Title.   II. Series.
   Z52.5.M52R547   1990
   652.5'536--dc20

                         90-26960
                           CIP

Printed and bound in the United States of America.

1 2 3 4 5 6 7 8 9 RARA 4 3 2 1

Distributed to the book trade in Canada by Macmillan of Canada, a division of
Canada Publishing Corporation.

Distributed to the book trade outside the United States and Canada by Penguin
Books Ltd.

Penguin Books Ltd., Harmondsworth, Middlesex, England
Penguin Books Australia Ltd., Ringwood, Victoria, Australia
Penguin Books N.Z. Ltd., 182–190 Wairau Road, Auckland 10, New Zealand

British Cataloging-in-Publication Data available.

Acquisitions Editor: Marjorie Schlaikjer
Project Editor: Megan E. Sheppard
Technical Editor: Gerald Joyce

Contents

Introduction

Microsoft Word 5.5 can be easy to use, but there is a lot to learn—and a lot you probably don't need to learn as long as you can look it up quickly. This alphabetic guide is designed to help you use features as you need them. Merely look up a task and find simple, direct instructions.

For example, to learn or remember how to draw lines, look up Lines. To clear a document from the screen, look up Clearing a document. To get all the information you need but don't want to remember about the expanded macro language in version 5.5, look up Macros. Most entries provide hands-on instructions, but some entries—such as Style sheets—explain a concept or provide a framework for your understanding.

If you're new to Word 5.5, look first at these topics: Starting Word, Commands, Dialog box, Opening a document, Selecting text, Built-in formats, Printing, Saving a document, and Exiting Word.

Absolute positioning

Absolute positioning is a desktop publishing technique. It lets you position a paragraph (containing text or graphics) at a specific place on a page. Once a paragraph is positioned, other text that is not positioned will "flow" around it, changing line length as necessary. For example, you can place a boxed paragraph or a chart in the center of a page or across two of a page's three columns and let other text flow around it without any special effort on your part.

To position a paragraph in this way, first select (highlight) any part of the paragraph and then choose Format Position (Alt+TO). Set the following fields of the dialog box as appropriate, and press Enter.

1

Horizontal Where do you want the paragraph positioned on the page horizontally (from left to right)? Type a number for a specific distance, such as *2.2"* or *12 cm*, or use the Down direction key to select from Left, Centered, Right, Inside (to the left on odd-numbered pages and to the right on even-numbered pages), and Outside (the opposite of Inside). Your choice is measured relative to the next field.

Relative to Do you want the horizontal position measured in relation to the *Margins, Page,* or *Column?*

Vertical Where do you want the paragraph positioned on the page vertically (from top to bottom)? As with the Horizontal field, type a number for a specific distance, or press the Down direction key to see a list. Word's proposed response in this field is *In line,* which means the paragraph prints immediately after the paragraph that precedes it in the document. The other choices available when you press Down are Top, Centered, and Bottom.

Relative to Do you want the vertical position measured in relation to the margins of the page or the page edges?

Distance from Text How much blank space do you want around the outside of the paragraph's frame? The default is .167", equivalent to one standard line (⅙ inch). This setting affects the left and right sides of the paragraph frame only if the value of the Paragraph Width field is narrower than the width of the default text column. It affects the top and bottom of the paragraph frame only if the value of the Vertical field is something other than In line.

Paragraph Width How much elbow room do you want the printable content of the paragraph to have? By reducing the width of a paragraph's frame, you allow room for other text to flow around the paragraph. The default, Single Column, causes the paragraph frame to use the full width of the column (which is from margin to margin in a single-column document). If you type a number (such as *3"*), only a region that wide will be "positioned"—freeing other text to flow into any extra space outside the paragraph frame. If you press the Down direction key or Alt+Down, the resulting list of choices includes the default Single Column as well as Width of Graphic, which makes the paragraph's frame as wide as the graphic image contained in the paragraph. For a multicolumn page, you see the additional choices Double Column (twice the column width) and Between Margins (the width of the printed page between the left and right margins). You can even make a frame wider than the column, causing the contents of the paragraph to extend into a page margin.

Most results of Format Position are invisible until you print or use File Print Preview.

See also: Capture; Frames; Layout techniques; Linking graphics; Paragraph formatting; Section formatting.

Accelerator key

See: Dialog box.

Adding numbers

See: Math.

Advanced Quick Help

See: MasterWord Help.

Allsave

In Word 5.0, the Transfer Allsave command saved all files to disk. In Word 5.5, this is accomplished with File Save All (Alt+FE).

See: Saving all files.

Alphabetizing

See: Sorting.

Annotations

An annotation is a special kind of footnote used for insertion of editorial comments or questions into a document. Annotations are automatically numbered, just as footnotes can be, but unlike normal footnotes they also can contain the initials (or other mark) of the person who wrote them. This lets a reader identify the source of each comment.

To place your first comment in a document, select (highlight) the point at which you want the comment to appear, choose Insert Annotation (Alt+IA), and type your initials in the Annotation Mark field. To include the current date and time as part of the annotation, choose Yes in the Include Date and Include Time fields. Press Enter, and Word instantly inserts an annotation reference mark and moves to the end of the document, where annotation text and other footnote text is stored. Type your comment, and then use Edit Go To (Alt+EG or F5) to return to the annotation mark in the main body of the document.

Once you have used Insert Annotation, you can choose the command and press Enter immediately; you needn't fill in the fields, because Word will remember your mark (initials) and whether you want the date and time as part of the annotation.

In most regards, an annotation is like any other footnote. (For example, you can view footnotes and annotations together in a special window pane that is activated with the View menu's Footnotes/Annotations command.) However,

because you probably will want to print a final draft of
your document without annotations showing, you might
want to format the annotations and their reference marks
(such as your initials) in hidden text. The easiest way to do
this is by using a style sheet, formatting the Annotation Ref
character style and the Annotation paragraph style with
hidden text. Then use the Hidden Text check box in the
Print Options dialog box (File menu) to control whether the
text prints.

See also: Footnotes; Hidden text; Styles.

Applying a style

To apply a style to text, thereby formatting the text according to the style's instructions, first select (highlight) the
text and then use one of the following three methods:

Key Code
If you know the style's key code, hold down the Ctrl key
and press Y, then release Ctrl and type the one-character or
two-character key code. This is the preferred way to apply
a style as long as you don't have a conflicting macro—a
macro that has a control code beginning with Ctrl+Y.
Alternatively, you can hold down the Shift and Ctrl keys
and type the key code; unfortunately, this creates conflicts
with macros, which often use Shift+Ctrl codes and which
override styles when competing for the same code. After a
style has been applied to a paragraph or section, the style's
key code will appear in the style bar, if you've turned on
the style bar with the View menu's Preferences dialog box.

Apply Style Command
Another way to apply a style, regardless of whether you remember its key code, is with the Format menu's Apply
Style command (Alt+TY). Choose the command and, if
you remember the key code, type it into the Key Code text

box of the Apply Style dialog box. If you do not remember the key code, choose the desired style by name from the list box that appears in the center of the dialog box. Initially, this list box contains only paragraph styles, but you can change the listing to either Character or Section styles by adjusting the Style Type drop-down list box.

Ribbon

Although it can't be used to apply a character or section style, the ribbon provides you with an excellent way to apply a paragraph style to text. Press Ctrl+S to highlight the Style drop-down list box, or Ctrl+SS to bring the Apply Style dialog box to the screen. Move through the existing list of styles either by pressing the Down direction key or by pressing Alt+Down.

Comments

Deliberately applying dedicated styles is unnecessary. For example, the dedicated Paragraph Footnote style applies itself to footnote text. However, if you want a style applied to a kind of text to which it's not dedicated, you must do it yourself.

See also: Key codes; Ribbon; Styles; Style sheets.

ASCII files

Word allows you to open and save ASCII files—files in which all special formatting characters have been removed.

Opening

To open an ASCII file, use File Open (Alt+FO or Alt+ Ctrl+F2) and type the full name of the file, including the extension (unless the extension is the default, .DOC). If the file has no extension, type the first part of the name followed by a period.

Some ASCII files have a paragraph mark (¶) at the end of each line. The screen shows paragraph marks if the

Paragraph Marks check box is turned on in the View
menu's Preferences dialog box. Word needs paragraph
marks only at the ends of paragraphs. Delete unwanted
paragraph marks, either individually or with Edit Replace.

Saving

To save an ASCII file with a paragraph mark (carriage
return/linefeed) at the end of each paragraph only, choose
File Save As (Alt+FA or Alt+F2), and choose Text Only in
the Format list box.

If you want paragraph marks at the end of each line, choose
File Save As (Alt+FA or Alt+F2), and choose Text Only
w/Breaks in the Format list box.

If you want to create a second copy of your Word file, with
or without line breaks, but retain your document in Word
format as well, give the file a new name before saving it.

See also: List box; Paragraph mark.

Asterisk

See: Outlining; Style bar; Wildcards.

Attaching a style sheet

If the document is displayed on the screen, choose the Format menu's Attach Style Sheet command (Alt+TA), and
then either type the name of the style sheet or highlight it
in the Files list box. Be sure the Attach option is selected,
and then press Enter.

See also: Detaching a style sheet; Style sheets.

AUTOEXEC

AUTOEXEC is a name given to sets of instructions that
automatically execute.

In Word, a macro named AUTOEXEC executes as soon as
the glossary file (.GLY file) containing the macro is loaded
into Word. If the AUTOEXEC macro is included in a
NORMAL.GLY file, the macro executes as soon as Word
is started.

In DOS, an AUTOEXEC.BAT file is a batch file containing DOS commands. If it is in the same directory as
COMMAND.COM, AUTOEXEC.BAT executes whenever
you start or reboot your computer. (DOS first executes the
instructions in the CONFIG.SYS file, then loads the
COMMAND.COM file, and then executes the AUTO-
EXEC.BAT file.)

A typical AUTOEXEC.BAT file on a fixed disk (here
named drive C) might contain the following DOS commands, each on a separate line. This line tells DOS where
to look for programs:

```
path=c:\word;c:\dos;c:\bat
```

This line changes the DOS prompt to show directory as
well as drive:

```
prompt=$p$g
```

This line sets up serial port 1 for certain serial printers:

```
mode com1:96,n,8,1,p
```

This line enables Word to better print long, complex documents on a printer connected to the first parallel port:

```
mode lpt1:,,p
```

To have Word start each time you start your computer,
make the last line of an AUTOEXEC.BAT file *word*. If you
want Word to always load the last document you were
working on, make the last line *word/l*.

To use Word to create an AUTOEXEC.BAT file, type the commands one to a line, choose File Save As (Alt+FA or Alt+F2) and type the name *AUTOEXEC.BAT*, and then move to the Format list box and choose Text Only. Press Enter, and then press Enter again when Word prompts *Saving 'Text Only' will result in loss of formatting*.

See also: CONFIG.SYS; DOS commands; Macros; Mode; Mouse; Printing.

Automatic styles

Certain styles in a style sheet are dedicated to particular tasks, and Word uses them unless otherwise instructed. For example, if you create a Paragraph Normal style in a style sheet, Word formats most paragraphs with it unless you deliberately apply other formatting. Similarly, a Normal Section style formats the layout of pages in any section not explicitly formatted in some other way. There is no Character Normal style because the character component of the Paragraph Normal style governs a document's default character formatting.

Character Styles

The automatic character styles are Character Page Number, which formats page numbers; Character Line Number, which formats line numbers; Character Footnote Ref, which formats footnote reference marks; Character Annotation Ref, which formats annotation reference marks; Character Line Draw, which lets you control the font and font size used for printing line-drawing characters; and Character Summary Info, which formats summary information.

Paragraph Styles

The automatic paragraph styles are Paragraph Normal, which formats all paragraphs not otherwise formatted; Paragraph Header/Footer, which formats headers and footers; Paragraph Footnotes, which formats footnotes (but not

footnote reference marks); Paragraph Annotation, which
formats the text of annotation footnotes (but not annotation
reference marks); Paragraph Heading level (1 through 7),
seven styles that format levels of headings; Paragraph Index
level (1 through 4), four styles that format levels of index
entries; and Paragraph Table level (1 through 4), four styles
that format levels of entries in tables of contents.

Section Style

The sole dedicated section style is Normal Section, which
formats the layout of pages unless other section formatting
is present.

Autosave

To instruct Word to make periodic backup copies (on disk)
of the documents, style sheets, and other files on which you
are working, choose the Utilities menu's Customize command (Alt+UU) and type a number in the Autosave Frequency box. This number represents the number of minutes
Word will wait between saves. If you type *0* or leave the
field blank, the autosave feature is turned off.

To have Word check with you before saving in this way,
turn on the Confirm check box.

The autosave feature is not what it might appear at first. It
is not a version of the Save command that triggers itself.
Rather, the autosave feature creates special files on disk
that have the extensions .SVD, .SVG, and .SVS. When you
quit Word, the files are erased; you needn't give them a
second thought. But if power is lost to your computer, or if
for some other reason you lose work in progress, the .SVD,
.SVG, and .SVS files are not erased. Consequently, Word
detects the files at startup and asks whether you want your
document(s), style sheet(s), and glossary file(s) to be updated with information from the .SVD, .SVG, and .SVS
files. The message is: *Autosave back up files exist. Do you
want to recover files now?*

Turning on the autosave feature does not replace your need
to save your documents (using Save), your style sheets
(using the style sheet window's Save command), or your
glossary entries (using the Save Glossary command). But it
does provide backup protection...just in case.

See also: Saving a document.

Boilerplate text

See: Glossary.

Bold characters

To format characters as bold, first select (highlight) the
characters, and then use one of these three methods:

Format Character
Choose Format Character (Alt+TC), turn on the Bold check
box, and press Enter.

Built-In Format
Hold down Ctrl and press B. If your glossary contains a
macro whose control code begins with Ctrl+B, hold down
Ctrl and press AB.

Styles
If a style sheet is attached to your document and it includes
a character style for boldface, press Ctrl+Y and type the
one-character or two-character key code of the style, such
as BC (for Bold Character). To see which styles are available in a style sheet, choose Format Apply Styles (Alt+TY)
and choose Character in the Style Type field, or choose
Format Define Styles (Alt+TD) to look in the style sheet
window.

To type in bold text, use any of these three methods before typing.

Comments

Although you can format characters as bold, they won't print that way unless your printer and .PRD file are able to print bold.

See also: Applying a style; Built-in formats; Character formatting; Key codes; Printer files; Styles; Style sheet window.

Bookmarks

To place a "bookmark" in a document so that you can instantly find the section of the document later, select (highlight) the text that you want to mark and then choose the Insert menu's Bookmark command (Alt+IM). Type a name for the bookmark, and press Enter.

A bookmark name can be up to 31 characters in length, but cannot contain spaces. To separate words within a name, use hyphens, periods, underlines, or capitalization.

To return to bookmarked text later, choose Edit Go To (Alt+EG), select the Bookmark option, and either type the name of the bookmark or choose it from the Bookmark Name list box. Then press Enter.

To incorporate a copy of a bookmarked passage in a different document, highlight the point at which you want the copy to appear and use Insert File (Alt+IF).

In order to make a cross-reference to a passage, you must first mark it with a bookmark.

See also: Cross-references; Jumping through a document; Linking documents.

Borders and boxes around paragraphs

See: Lines; Paragraph formattin

Borders on the screen

See: Window borders.

Built-in formats

To use a built-in character format, first select (highlight) the characters, and then hold down Ctrl and type the letter corresponding to the built-in character format. For example, Ctrl+B produces bold, Ctrl+U produces underlining, and Ctrl+I produces italics. Ctrl+Spacebar removes any special character formatting. Ctrl+Z removes special character formatting but does not change a character's font or size.

To use a built-in paragraph format, place the cursor in the paragraph to be formatted, or select at least one character from the paragraphs to be formatted, hold down Ctrl, and type the letter corresponding to the built-in paragraph format. For example, Ctrl+C centers lines and Ctrl+O opens paragraph spacing—that is, produces a blank line before each paragraph. Ctrl+X removes special paragraph formatting.

If a macro in your glossary uses Ctrl plus a letter as its code, and if the letter is already used in a built-in format, you must hold down Ctrl and press A followed by the letter.

(Holding down A is necessary only if the built-in format has as its letter the first letter of a macro's control code. To sidestep this problem, you should assign to macros control codes that begin with Shift+Ctrl instead of Ctrl.)

The Appendix lists built-in character and paragraph formats.

See also: Selecting text.

Buttons

See: Command buttons.

Calculations

See: Math.

Canceling a command

To cancel a command in progress, press the Esc key.

See also: Commands.

Capitalizing

See: Changing case.

Capture

Capture is a DOS program that comes with Word. It allows images from the computer screen to be captured so that they can be imported into Word documents. It will not work with OS/2, not even in DOS compatibility mode.

To install Capture the first time, change to the directory containing CAPTURE.COM, type *capture/s*, and use the menu that appears to set options as desired. During future computing sessions you need type only *capture* to install the program. (The options settings from before will be remembered.)

To use Capture once it has been installed, hold down the Shift key and press the Print Screen key, type a name for the image you are capturing, and press Enter. In most circumstances, you will be able to crop the image at this point by pressing the direction keys to move crop marks across the screen. The Tab key lets you move from one crop mark to another. When the image is cropped as desired, press the Enter key again.

To import an image into a Word document, use Insert Picture. In most cases, you then will want to use Format Position to refine the final look and location of the graphic in your document.

There are a large number of wrinkles, warnings, and considerations involved in the use of Capture. For details, refer to pages 399 to 402 of the manual *Using Microsoft Word*.

See also: Absolute positioning; Filenames and extensions; Linking graphics.

Carriage-return key

See: Enter key.

Centering

To center the line or lines of a paragraph, first place the
cursor in the paragraph and then use one of these three
methods:

Format Paragraph

Choose Format Paragraph (Alt+TP), set the Alignment
field to Center, and press Enter.

Built-In Format

Hold down Ctrl and press C. If a macro is in use that uses
Ctrl+C or Ctrl+C and another character as its code, use the
built-in format by holding down Ctrl and pressing AC.

Styles

If a style sheet is attached to your document and it includes
a paragraph style for centering, press Ctrl+Y and type the
style's one-character or two-character key code.

You can also use Format Position to absolutely position a
paragraph at the center of a page or column. This method
allows vertical as well as horizontal centering.

See also: Absolute positioning; Applying a style; Built-in
formats; Key codes; Paragraph formatting; Styles; Style
sheet window.

Changing case

To make a lowercase letter an uppercase letter, or vice
versa, you can always retype the letter. (Either delete and
retype, or use overtype mode.) However, two faster
methods do exist.

With the first method, you can use the All Caps field of the
Format menu's Character dialog box to instruct Word to
format all selected characters as uppercase. Unless these

letters are typed as capita   ey will remain lowercase in
content, but this will be   a secret, since Word will
display and print them a: als because of their formatting. They will be lower   etters in disguise, so to speak.

The second method is to   t (highlight) the letter or letters and then hold down   hift key and press F3. If a
single character is select   the time, its case will change.
If multiple characters ar   cted, Word follows a specific
formula: If the first sele   character is lowercase, all
characters become uppe   ; if every character is uppercase, all characters but tne first character of each word
become lowercase; if only the first character of the selection, or of some or all of the words, is uppercase, all characters become lowercase. If nothing is selected—if the
cursor is inside a word but nothing is highlighted, for
example—Word acts as if the entire word were selected.
This formula is powerful and fast. For example, as you
press Shift+F3 a succession of times, *this* becomes *THIS*
becomes *This* becomes *this* again.

See also: Character formatting; Overtyping.

Changing tabs

See: Tabs.

Character formatting

Character formatting controls the font, the size, and other
attributes of characters, such as boldfacing, underlining,
and superscripting.

To format characters already typed, first select (highlight)
the characters and then use one of the following three

methods. To format characters before they are typed, first
use one of these methods and then type the text.

Format Character

Choose Format Character (Alt+TC), set the following fields
of the dialog box as appropriate, and press Enter:

Font In what font (shape of type) do you want to print the
text? Press Alt+Down to see a list of the possibilities
allowed by the .PRD file.

Point Size What size do you want the text to be? Press
Alt+Down to see a list of sizes allowed by the .PRD file.

Color What color do you want text to be printed in?
(Black is usually the only choice, unless your printer uses
multiple colors.) This field does not affect the color in
which text appears on screen.

Bold Do you want the text in boldface?

Italic Do you want the text in italics?

Underline Do you want the text underlined?

Double Underline Do you want the text underlined twice?

Small Kaps Do you want the lowercase letters displayed
and printed in smaller-than-normal capital letters?

All Caps Do you want the text displayed and printed in all
capital letters?

Strikethru Do you want a horizontal line struck through
the text?

Hidden Do you want text to be formatted as ''hidden''?
(Whether ''hidden'' text really is hidden on your screen is
governed by the View menu's Preferences dialog box, and
whether it prints is governed by the File menu's Print Options dialog box.)

Position Do you want the text displayed and printed normally, slightly above the line (superscript), or below the
line (subscript)?

Built-In Format

Hold down Ctrl and press the letter of a built-in character
format. For example, hold down Ctrl and press B for bold.
If your glossary contains a macro whose control code
begins with Ctrl+B, use Ctrl+AB to apply the built-in format for boldface.

For a complete list of built-in character formats, see the
Appendix.

Styles

If a style sheet is attached to your document and it includes
a character style for the formatting you want, press Ctrl+Y
and type the one-character or two-character key code of the
style, such as BC (for Bold Character). To see which styles
are available in a style sheet, choose Format Apply Styles
(Alt+TY) and choose Character in the Style Type field, or
choose Format Define Styles (Alt+TD) to look in the style
sheet window.

Comments

Your .PRD file and printer govern the availability of
specific character formatting alternatives.

See also: Applying a style; Built-in formats; Changing
case; Colors on the screen; Downloadable fonts; Key codes;
Printer files; Ribbon; Styles; Style sheet window.

Check boxes

A check box option in a dialog box—represented by [ ]—
offers a simple on or off choice. If an *X* appears in the box,
then the option is *on*; if the box is empty, then the option is
off. To turn the option on or off, press the Spacebar.

Clearing a document

See: Closing a window.

Clearing tabs

See: Tabs.

Click

See: Mouse.

Clipboard

If you're using Word for DOS under Microsoft Windows /286, Windows /386, or Windows 3 in 386 Enhanced mode, the permanent glossary name *clipboard* will appear in Edit Glossary's list of glossary entries. As with other permanent glossary entries, such as *date* and *time,* you cannot edit or delete this glossary entry, only use it.

In Windows, the clipboard functions as an intermediary between various programs, providing a temporary storage place for information being transferred from one document or application to another. Word's *clipboard* glossary entry gives you the ability to transfer text to and from Windows applications or to insert some graphics from a Windows application by passing the graphics through the Windows clipboard.

To use the *clipboard* glossary entry, type the word *clipboard* into your document at the place where you want to insert the contents of the clipboard, and then press the F3 key. If you are importing graphics images into Word through the Windows clipboard, you can use Insert Picture as well as the glossary if the images are contained in a file.

Any graphics you want to transfer from a Windows application into Word through the clipboard must be "bit-mapped"—stored pixel by pixel (more or less, this means dot by dot). Windows also recognizes another type of graphic that is stored in a form called a "metafile." In a metafile, the graphic itself is not saved as a picture, like a bitmap, but the instructions that create it are saved. These instructions are used by a program to redraw the image on the screen or on paper. Word cannot handle metafiles, so before you try to move a graphics image by means of the *clipboard* glossary name, check the documentation for the image-drawing program to determine whether its files are saved as bitmaps or as metafiles. Some programs, such as Microsoft Excel, create either metafiles or bitmaps.

Comments

The *clipboard* glossary entry is not available if you are running Windows 3 in real or standard mode. You must be in enhanced mode, which requires a 386-based or 486-based computer with at least 2 megabytes of memory. To import graphics from Windows, use the Windows Paintbrush application to save clipboard graphics as .PCX files, and then use Insert Picture to import the graphics image. To import text from the Windows clipboard, switch to Windows and then use the Paste command.

See also: Glossary; Linking graphics.

Closing a document

See: Closing a window.

Closing all files

To close all files, including glossary and style sheet files
as well as document files and their associated windows,
choose File Close All (Alt+FL). If you have edited any
files since the last time you saved them, Word will prompt
you to save changes to each in turn.

Closing a window

Unlike in earlier versions of Word, by closing a document
in Word 5.5 you also close its associated window. You can
thus remove a text window from the screen by choosing
File Close (Alt+FC) or Window Close (Alt+WC). If you
have edited the document since the last time you saved it,
Word will ask *Do you want to save changes to (filename)?*

Both of these commands apply to the active window only.

See also: Windows.

Colors on the screen

Assuming you have a color monitor, you can exercise ex-
tensive control over the colors that appear on the screen.
Simply choose View Preferences (Alt+VE), and choose the
Colors command button. The Colors dialog box appears.

A series of letters appears to the right, each with a different
color next to it. This is your palette of possibilities. In the
list box at the left are the names of screen elements, such as
menus, borders, and messages. To assign a color to an element, use the direction keys to select (highlight) the name

of the element, and then press Alt plus the letter corresponding to the desired color. The contents of the small box
below the list box change to the chosen color, allowing you
to examine your color choice. To change colors, simply
press a different letter. Select colors for as many elements
as you desire, and then press Enter. Word remembers your
choices for future editing sessions.

■ If you operate in a graphics mode, character formatting
   is depicted on the screen. (That is, italics are italicized,
   bold characters are bold, and so on.) You can adjust the
   color of 21 on-screen elements, but text always will display in the same color.

■ If you operate in a text (nongraphics) mode, color can be
   used to reflect character formatting. For example, bold
   text can be red, italic text blue, and bold italics yellow,
   if you like. In text mode, you can assign colors to 18
   kinds and combinations of character formatting, in addition to the screen elements (such as borders) for which
   you can adjust colors whether you are in a graphics
   mode or a text mode.

Sometimes characters are formatted in such a way that two
different colors are appropriate. In such cases, Word must
choose which color to display. It uses the following priority
list, with formatting attributes listed earlier given precedence over later attributes: font size, hidden text, subscript,
superscript, strikethrough, small cap, uppercase, double
underline, italic and underline together, bold and italic
together, bold and underline together, underline, italic,
bold, and normal (no special formatting). In other words,
if a font is both small and bold, it is displayed in the color
specified for small type rather than in the color for bold
type, because "font size" comes before "bold" on the list.
You can alter Word's priority list by telling it to remove a
particular character attribute from the list. Do this by highlighting the name of the attribute (such as "font 8.5 pts or
less") and pressing Alt+R. In this example, text that was
both bold and small (8.5 pts or less) would be displayed in
the color listed for bold rather than in the color for small
fonts.

To control whether you are in a graphics mode or a text mode, choose View Preferences, move to the Display Mode option, and press Alt+Down to see a scrollable list of the modes available on your system. To switch between the two modes that you have most recently used, hold down the Alt key and press F9.

See also: Character formatting; Display mode; View Preferences.

Columns, moving

To move a column that is part of a table, first select (high-light) it. This involves turning on the column selection mode by holding down the Shift and Ctrl keys, pressing F8, and using the direction keys or mouse to highlight the column. Then delete it to the scrap. Now move the cursor (selection) to the upper-left corner of the area where you want to insert the column, and press Shift+Ins. You might want to turn on the Tabs check box of the View menu's Preferences dialog box so that tab characters are displayed; this makes it easier to move a column of tab characters, should you need to.

See also: Scrap; Selecting a column.

Columns, multiple

To format a document to print in multiple columns on a page, choose Format Section (Alt+TS) and type a number in the Number text box. To adjust the spacing between columns, type a number in the Spacing text box (the default is 0.5"). Then press Enter.

To create a boundary between parts of your document that are to have different numbers of columns, insert a section

break by choosing Insert Break (Alt+IB), choosing Column
in the first field, and then pressing Enter. You can change
the number of columns in the middle of a page. This involves setting the Type of Section Break field of the Break
dialog box to Continuous.

For greater flexibility (but at the expense of more work on
your part), use side-by-side paragraphs to create columns.

See also: Section formatting; Section mark; Side-by-side
text.

Command buttons

A command button is a dialog-box choice that is enclosed
in angle brackets. Choosing such a button (by pressing Alt
followed by the accelerator key, by pressing the Tab key
until the button is highlighted and then pressing Enter, or
by clicking on it with the mouse) performs an action. The
OK command button executes the command; the Cancel
command button closes the dialog box and cancels the command; and command buttons followed by an ellipsis (...)
lead to another dialog box.

Command fields

See: Dialog box.

Commands

To use a command, press Alt or F10 to move from the
document area (also called text area) to the menu bar at the
top of the screen. (If the menu hasn't been visible, it

appears when you press Alt or F10.) Choose a family of
commands by pressing the accelerator key (the emphasized
letter, a letter that is either boldfaced or in a different color)
of one of the nine names appearing on the menu bar. This
causes a drop-down menu to appear, listing the commands
in that family. To choose one of these commands, press its
accelerator key.

For example, to use the Format menu's Section command,
press Alt+TS—the Alt to activate the menu bar, T to activate the Format drop-down menu, and S to activate the
Section command.

You can also choose a command by highlighting it on the
menu and pressing Enter or by clicking the mouse on first
the menu name and then the command itself.

Some commands execute as soon as they are chosen.
Others, shown on the drop-down menus with an ellipsis
(...) after their names, require you to choose options in a
dialog box before pressing Enter to carry out the command.

To leave the menu bar without carrying out a command,
press Esc or click the left mouse button when the mouse
pointer is in the document area.

See also: Dialog box; Drop-down menu.

CONFIG.SYS

CONFIG.SYS is an optional file that configures DOS
when you start or reboot your computer. It must be in the
root directory of the disk from which you start DOS (drive
C in most fixed-disk systems).

For example, a typical CONFIG.SYS file might contain instructions similar to the following. This line sets the maximum number of memory buffers to 20:

```
buffers=20
```

This line increases the maximum number of files or devices that can be opened concurrently (should be set to at least 15 if you want to use Word's spell-checker):

```
files=20
```

This line installs the software driver for the Microsoft mouse, assuming the file MOUSE.SYS is in the C:\ directory:

```
device=c:\mouse.sys
```

(Alternatively, you can install the mouse with the MOUSE.COM program by typing *MOUSE* at the DOS prompt.)

The CONFIG.SYS file is also where you put instructions that create "RAM disks" (not real disks at all, but portions of random access memory set aside to be used as if they were disks), access multiple fixed disks or CD-ROM drives, configure your keyboard for a country other than the United States, and so forth. See your DOS manual for additional information.

To create a CONFIG.SYS file with Word, type the instructions one to a line, choose File Save As (Alt+FS) and type the name *CONFIG.SYS*, move to the Format list box and choose Text Only, press Enter, and then choose OK (press Enter) when Word asks you to confirm the loss of formatting.

See also: AUTOEXEC; Mouse.

Context-sensitive help

See: Help; MasterWord Help.

Control codes

To use a control code to run a specific macro, hold down Ctrl or Shift and Ctrl, and type the one-character or two-character code. For example, if a macro's control code is Shift+Ctrl+BP, hold down the Shift and Ctrl keys, and press B. Then release the Shift and Ctrl keys and press P.

If you create a macro, assign a control code to it at that time. If you are using Macro Record, assign a control code (in the Macro Keys text box) before you begin recording. If you are defining a macro which you have written as text, assign a control code in the Macro Keys text box of the Edit Macro dialog box. Hold down Ctrl (or Shift+Ctrl) and press the first character of the key code. Then release Ctrl (or Shift+Ctrl) and type the second letter.

Generally, two-letter control codes are better than one-letter codes because the total number of possible codes is increased. (The same is true of key codes for use with formatting styles.) Also, it is best to begin key codes with Shift+Ctrl (rather than just Ctrl); this helps keep your control codes from conflicting with formatting operations that use the Ctrl key.

You can assign new purposes to function keys by creating a macro that performs the desired task and then assigning a function key as the macro's control code. This is true whether you press the function key alone or use it in combination with Ctrl, Shift, or Alt. For example, to make Alt+F8 perform some special task, create a macro that performs the task and use Alt+F8 as its control code. In this case, if you want to gain access to the former function of the Alt+F8 key combination, which is to select a sentence, use Ctrl+A followed by Alt+F8.

Note: *A control code runs a macro or inserts a text entry from the glossary; a key code applies a style from a style sheet.*

See also: Function keys; Key codes; Macros.

Copying formatting

You can copy formatting from one location to another in a variety of ways. The most elegant and flexible is to record a style, thereby saving the desired formatting instructions in a style sheet. If you're not using a style sheet, several other approaches are available.

Copying a Paragraph Mark or a Section Mark

Each paragraph ends in a (usually invisible) paragraph mark that stores the paragraph's formatting instructions. (You can control the visibility of the paragraph marks by using the Paragraph Marks check box in the Preferences dialog box of the View menu.) Each section of a multiple-section document ends in a section mark that stores the section's page-layout formatting. To copy paragraph or section formatting from one location to another, select (highlight) the appropriate mark, and choose Edit Copy (Alt+EC) to copy it to the scrap. Now move to the end of the paragraph or section that is to receive the formatting, delete its paragraph or section mark (not to the scrap), then hold down Shift and press Ins. Doing so inserts the new, properly formatted mark.

Using F4

To copy character, paragraph, or section formatting, first select a sample of text that is formatted as desired. Next choose the command from the Format menu that is appropriate for the formatting you want to copy. For example, to copy character formatting, choose Format Character (Alt+TC); to copy paragraph formatting, choose Format Paragraph (Alt+TP). After choosing the command, press Enter without making any changes in the dialog box. Next, select text that you want to format to match the sample, and press F4.

Using the Mouse

To copy character formatting with the mouse, first select the passage to be formatted. Now move the mouse pointer outside the selection to a single character that is formatted the way you want; hold down Ctrl and Shift and click the left mouse button.

To copy paragraph formatting with the mouse, first select the paragraph(s) to be formatted. Now move the mouse pointer to the selection bar at the left of a paragraph that is formatted the way you want; hold down Ctrl and Shift and click the left mouse button. (If you're in graphics mode, the mouse pointer points to the right when it is in the selection bar.)

See also: Glossary; Mouse; Recording a style; Selection bar.

Copying text to the glossary

See: Glossary.

Copying text to the scrap

You can copy text to the scrap, a temporary holding area that is represented on the bottom line of the screen by two brackets { }. You can then insert the text at a different location in the same document or in a different document.

To copy text to the scrap, select the text and hold down Alt and press F3 or choose Edit Copy (Alt+EC). To insert the passage from the scrap into a document, select the location for the insertion and choose Edit Paste (Alt+EP).

See also: Deleting text; Glossary; Moving text; Scrap.

Counting words

Count the number of words in a document using Utilities Word Count. If no text is selected, Word Count counts all the words in the document. If text is selected, only the words in the selection are counted.

You can also obtain a word count by using Utilities Spelling, but that tells you the number of words for which spelling was checked rather than the number of words in the document. The number differs because the spell-checker ignores one-letter and two-letter words.

MasterWord includes a macro that counts both the number of words in a document and the number of words from the beginning of the document to the cursor location.

Creating a style sheet

See: Styles; Style sheet window.

Cross-references

To create cross-references in a document, you must first understand how to use bookmarks and how to number using a series name and the F3 key. Once you have these skills, cross-referencing becomes a simple matter of typing a series name followed by a colon and a bookmark name, and pressing the F3 key.

Three series names are built into Word, making common types of cross-references easy to use. These built-in names are *page, footnote,* and *paragraph.* The following example clarifies their use.

If you want to write *See the discussion of "love handles" on page X* but you don't know what page number to use, first highlight the discussion and give it a bookmark name (such as *flab*). Then go to the sentence ending *...on page X*, but instead of typing *X*, type *page:flab* and press F3. In this case, *page* is the built-in series name, and *flab* is the bookmark name. When you print the document, the number of the page that begins the discussion marked *flab* is inserted as a cross-reference at the end of the sentence.

See also: Bookmarks; Numbering.

Cursor

The cursor is the little highlight you move around the screen. The cursor serves two purposes:

■ It indicates where the next text you type will be inserted.

■ It expands, allowing you to select text—a word, a phrase, a line, a paragraph, a column, or any other amount of text, including an entire document. Generally, you must select text before you act on it in some way, such as underlining it or deleting it.

See also: Selecting text.

Cut and paste

See: Moving text.

Dedicated styles

See: Automatic styles.

Defining a glossary entry

See: Glossary.

Deleting a document

See: File management (Delete).

Deleting a glossary entry

To delete a text entry from the glossary, choose Edit Glossary (Alt+EO) and from the Names list box select (highlight) the name of the entry you want to delete. Then choose the Delete command button. Doing so eliminates the entry from the copy of the glossary that is in the computer's active memory but doesn't affect the content of the glossary as it might exist on disk. You cannot delete the reserved glossary names (such as *page* and *date*).

See also: Deleting a macro; Glossary.

Deleting a macro

To delete a macro from the glossary, choose Macro Edit (Alt+ME) and from the Names list box select (highlight) the name of the entry you want to delete. Then choose the Delete command button. Doing so eliminates the entry from the copy of the glossary that is in the computer's active memory but doesn't affect the content of the glossary as it might exist on disk.

To delete the entry from the disk's copy of the glossary, choose Save Glossary. To retain the glossary in its previous form, type a new name for the edited version; otherwise, simply press Enter.

See also: Deleting a glossary entry; Glossary.

Deleting formatting

Word allows you to delete all three kinds of formatting: character, paragraph, and section.

Character

To remove special formatting, select (highlight) the character(s) and then hold down Ctrl and press the Spacebar.

If a style sheet is attached to the document, the use of Ctrl+Spacebar returns the selected characters to the formatting specified in the character portion of the paragraph governing the paragraph's formatting.

Paragraph

To remove formatting from a paragraph, move the cursor into the paragraph and then hold down Ctrl and press X.

If a macro in your glossary uses Ctrl+X as its control code or as the beginning of its control code, remove paragraph formatting by holding down Ctrl and pressing AX. You can also press Ctrl+Y followed by the key code for the Paragraph Normal style. (Typically, the key code for this style is NP.)

Section

To remove page-layout formatting from a document that has only a single section, move to the end of the document and delete the section mark that appears as a series of colons across the screen (::::::::::::::). When a document has more than one section, section marks are the boundaries between them, and deleting a section mark eliminates the page-layout formatting of the text that preceded it.

If a style sheet is attached to the document, you can return
to the style sheet's standard section formatting by pressing
Ctrl+Y followed by the key code for the Normal Section
style.

See also: Character formatting; Key codes; Paragraph formatting; Section formatting; Section mark; Styles; Style
sheets.

Deleting tabs

See: Tabs.

Deleting text

To delete text, select (highlight) the text and use the Del
key. What happens to the deleted text depends on the setting of Use INS for Overtype key in the Utilities menu's
Customize dialog box. If this option is checked, the
selected text is deleted to the scrap when Shift+Del is
pressed and deleted without being copied to the scrap when
Del is pressed. If this option is not checked, the selected
text is deleted to the scrap when Del is pressed and deleted
without being copied to the scrap when Shift+Del is
pressed.

See also: Copying text to the scrap; Glossary; Moving
text; Scrap.

Desktop publishing

See: Layout techniques.

Detaching a style sheet

To detach a style sheet from a document, either attach another style sheet or choose Format Attach Style Sheet (Alt+TA), press Del, and press Enter. Word asks *Do you want to convert style sheet formatting to direct formatting?* Choose *Yes* to retain the format of your document or *No* to discard all formatting that is controlled by the style sheet.

See also: Attaching a style sheet; NORMAL.STY; Styles; Style sheets.

Dialog box

When a menu command is followed by an ellipsis (...), choosing it will take you to a dialog box. The dialog box lets you specify how the command is to be carried out. You make your choices, and then usually you choose OK to put the command into effect. With a mouse, you choose OK by clicking on the OK button. With the keyboard, you generally press the Enter key since the OK button is usually selected by default. If you have used the Tab key, or sometimes a direction key, to select a command button other than the OK button, you must use the Tab key until the OK button is selected, and then press Enter. You can tell a button is selected because the angle brackets around it are highlighted or otherwise emphasized. A command can also be executed, and the dialog box closed, by choosing other command buttons.

To move among the choices offered in the dialog box, use the Tab key (Shift+Tab to move backward) or press Alt plus the emphasized key of the desired choice. This latter approach is known as using the accelerator key.

Each field in a dialog box is of one of the following types:

Text boxes You can type a choice into a text box. For example, you type a number into the Copies text box of the File menu's Print command. Sometimes a text box is linked to a list box so that any choice made in the list box is entered by Word into the text box. An example of this is the relationship between the File Name text box and the Files list box of the File menu's Open dialog box.

List boxes A list box lets you make a choice from a finite group of alternatives. As just noted, a choice in a list box sometimes is also expressed in a text box. In other instances, a choice made in a list box is reflected only in the list box itself. An example is the Printer Name list box of the File menu's Printer Setup dialog box.

Drop-down list box This looks like a text box but is distinguished visually by the downward-facing arrow at its right end. You can either press the Up or Down direction keys to scroll through the list of acceptable choices or, to see the list, hold down the Alt key and press the Down direction key, which drops down the list. Or, with a mouse, you click on the downward-facing arrow and then click on your choice from the resulting list.

Text/Drop-down list combo box This is a hybrid—part text box, part drop-down list box. It looks like a drop-down list box and can be used in the same manner: Use the Up and Down direction keys to select from a list, or use Alt+Down to show the list. It also works like a text box because you can type in a response, but only valid responses are accepted. An example is the Line Draw field in the Utilities menu's Customize dialog box.

Option buttons When a few mutually exclusive choices are available, Word often presents them as a box filled with option buttons. To make a choice, either use the Tab key to move to the box containing the option buttons and press the Spacebar until the one you want is selected, or else hold down the Alt key and press the appropriate accelerator key.

Check boxes Binary choices (yes/no or on/off) are made in check boxes. If the box has an *X* in it, it is set to *yes* or *on*. To change the setting of a check box, press the Tab key to move to it and then press the Spacebar. Or hold down the Alt key and press the appropriate accelerator key.

Command buttons At the bottom of each dialog box are its command buttons. The OK button carries out the command, in accordance with the choices made in the dialog box, and the Cancel button cancels it. Other command buttons will carry out different types of commands. In addition, there may be other command buttons with the names followed by an ellipsis (...). By choosing one of these buttons, you are taken to another dialog box to make related choices. Sometimes, though not often, command buttons take you to the main dialog box of another command.

When you have finished making choices in a dialog box, press Enter to carry out the selected command button, which is usually the OK button. Press Esc to cancel the dialog box (and the command).

See also: Check boxes; Command buttons; Drop-down list box; List box; Option buttons; Text box.

Diamond

See: End mark.

Dictionary

See: Spell-checking.

Directories and subdirectories

A directory is a portion of a disk that is treated as a separate entity, almost as if it were a disk itself.

Floppy disks generally have only a single directory, called the root directory, although you can create subdirectories on a floppy.

A well-organized hard disk almost invariably has multiple directories (the root directory and subdirectories, and often subdirectories of subdirectories). Using multiple directories, you can divide the large-capacity disk into smaller chunks that are dedicated to particular purposes. For example, you could store Word in a subdirectory called C:\WORD and business letters in a subdirectory called C:\LETTERS. Or you could store the letters in a subdirectory of the Word subdirectory: C:\WORD\LETTERS. If BALLET.DOC were a letter stored in such a subdirectory, its full name including drive and path would be C:\WORD\LETTERS\BALLET.DOC.

If the WORD subdirectory is in your DOS path, you can start Word from any directory on any disk. A good strategy is to start Word from the directory in which you want a document stored, though this directory may not stay active throughout your Word session.

To switch to a different directory before starting Word, use the DOS Change Directory (CD or CHDIR) command. See your DOS manual for information on this command as well as information on the Make Directory (MD or MKDIR) and Remove Directory (RD or RMDIR) commands.

Commands that ask you to type filenames (such as File Open and Insert File) present you with a list of files in the current directory (or on the current floppy disk). You can select (highlight) the desired filename in this list box; or press the Tab key to move to a Directories list box and highlight the name of a different drive or directory and press Enter to display its list of files. Select the [..] entry when you want to move up a level to a parent directory on the current drive.

See also: Opening a document; Path.

Display mode

Depending on your display adapter and monitor, Word can run in any of several modes. These modes fall into two broad categories: graphics and text. In graphics modes, character formatting is represented on the screen in a graphic way (for example, italics are italicized, super- scripts are small and raised, and so on), and the mouse pointer assumes shapes including that of an arrow. Text modes sacrifice some of this snazziness for greater speed and, sometimes, for greater visual clarity. In text modes, character formatting is reflected through the use of colors (on color monitors) or underlines (on monochrome monitors).

Systems that do not display graphics at all generally have only one mode. Most systems, however, allow a variety of modes—some graphics and some text. For the most part, these modes are distinguished by the number of lines they allow to be displayed on the screen. The normal screen has 25 lines, but some modes (on some systems) allow 43 or more lines.

The display modes Word makes available depend on choices you make when running Word's SETUP program. To choose among the modes, scroll through the options in the Display Mode field of the Preferences dialog box (View menu). To switch between the two display modes most re- cently used, hold down the Alt key and press F9.

See also: Character formatting; Colors on the screen; Mouse; View Preferences.

Dividing numbers

See: Math.

Division formatting

Unlike earlier versions, Word 5.5 no longer uses the term *division* to refer to page formatting. In Word 5.5, divisions are known as *sections*.

See: Section formatting.

Division mark

See: Section mark.

Document linking

See: Linking documents.

Document retrieval

See: File management.

DOS commands

To run a DOS command or another program without quitting Word, choose File DOS Commands (Alt+FD), type the command or program name, and press Enter. (On OS/2 systems the command is File OS/2 Commands.)

On a floppy-disk system, a message gives you a chance to replace the Word disk with another desired disk. When the command or program is done, you can press any key to return to Word.

You can run a succession of programs through File DOS Commands by "returning" to DOS first. Type *command* instead of a command or program name, and then press Enter. You see a DOS prompt (A>, C>), just as if you'd quit Word. In fact, Word is being held in memory. To return to Word, type *exit* at the DOS prompt, press Enter, and then press any key.

The first time you use File DOS Commands, Word proposes the name *command*. If that's the name you want, just press Enter. For subsequent uses of File DOS Commands, Word proposes the name you used previously.

A couple of warnings about using File DOS Commands. Don't run Word a second time by typing *word*. And don't load memory-resident programs such as Sidekick or the DOS Mode command. Although these programs might work fine with Word if loaded before Word is started, you can't load them *for the first time* through File DOS Commands.

One final tip: To provide additional memory to the program you're running through DOS, type the extension along with the filename when you run the command. For example, if you choose File DOS Commands and type *telecome.exe*, you might obtain better performance than if you simply typed *telecom*.

See also: AUTOEXEC; Mode; Path.

Double spacing

See: Paragraph formatting.

Downloadable fonts

A downloadable font is a set of instructions on disk that tells a laser printer how to create each character of a type-face—each character of a "font," in Word's parlance. When your printer is using a *bitmapped* font, a set of instructions must exist for each font size used in a document. With an *outline* or *scalable* font, only one set of instructions is needed because the printer adjusts ("scales") the size of the font. PostScript and some fonts for the HP LaserJet III are scalable.

To install your fonts, follow the instructions provided with them. (And be sure the instructions are valid for use with your version of Word.) To use a particular collection of fonts, including downloadable fonts, you must have an appropriate .PRD file and companion .DAT file. Word comes with a variety of .PRD and .DAT files for popular combinations of downloadable fonts. Some font installation programs even create .PRD files and .DAT files. In addition, you can merge existing .PRD files to create new ones; using Word's MERGEPRD program. More challenging is Word's MAKEPRD program, which lets you create or extensively modify .PRD files. To use either of these programs, refer to the Word documentation.

To actually use downloadable fonts, first install in the Printer Setup command's Printer File text box a .PRD file that supports the downloadable fonts you want. For example, if you use an HP LaserJet II, you might install HPDWNACP.PRD, which supports downloadable Helv and TmsRmn fonts in the sizes 6, 8, 10, 12, 14, 18, 24, and 30. This particular .PRD file supports the ASCII character set, which means that the characters it allows your printer to print are limited, more or less, to those you see on your keyboard. If instead you install the similarly named .PRD file, HPDWNADP.PRD, you get the same fonts and sizes and the Roman 8 character set, which has foreign and other characters—but which also takes up more disk space and more printer memory and takes more time to download.

After a .PRD file is installed, the Font and Point Size fields of the Format menu's Character dialog box will list the available fonts.

To keep Word from downloading the fonts before printing (to print faster), turn on the Skip Downloading Fonts check box in the Printer Setup dialog box (File menu).

See also: Character formatting; Mode; Printer files; Printing (Printer Setup).

Drop-down list box

At the right edge of some dialog box fields, you'll see a downward-facing arrow. Within these fields, you can hold down the Alt key and press the Down direction key, to see a drop-down list of available options. Choose one by highlighting it with the direction keys.

See also: Dialog box.

Drop-down menu

The menu bar at the top of the Word 5.5 screen lists nine
families of commands. When you press Alt to activate the
menu bar, one letter (the accelerator key) of each command
family name, or menu, becomes highlighted. Press one of
these keys to see the commands associated with the family.
This command list is called a "drop-down menu" because
it looks as if it is hanging down from the menu bar.

To choose a command from a drop-down menu, press its
accelerator key or select the command and press Enter. To
cancel the menu, press Esc.

See also: Commands.

End mark

Word marks the end of any document or style sheet with a
small diamond called the end mark. When you start a new
document, the only character that appears is this diamond,
because the beginning of a document that has no content is
also its end.

You cannot select (highlight), print, or format the end
mark. When you move the cursor to the end mark and then
type, text is inserted before the end mark; that is, the end
mark is pushed over or down to make room.

Unless you know Word well, avoid the end mark. When
you start a new document, press Enter a few times to move
the mark down and then press the Up direction key to move
away from it.

Enter key

To create a paragraph mark in a document, press Enter. To execute a command from a dialog box, press Enter when the OK button is active.

Erasing text

See: Deleting text.

Excel

See: Linking spreadsheets.

Exiting Word

To exit Word, choose File Exit Word (Alt+FX). If no documents or other files have unsaved editing, Word quits immediately. However, if changes to files would be lost as a result of exiting, Word displays the message *Do you want to save changes to (filename)?* Press *Y* to save the file and then quit; press *N* to quit without saving; press Esc to cancel the Exit Word command. If you press *Y* but the document hasn't yet been named, Word displays the Save As command's dialog box. After you name and save the document, Word exits to the operating system.

If there are unsaved changes to a style sheet or to the glossary, Word also asks if you want to save those changes before exiting.

Extending the selection

See: Selecting text.

Fields

See: Dialog box.

File management

To find and manipulate documents, use the File Management command on the File menu (Alt+FF). It lets you search for or view documents based on their name, directory, summary information, and content. It also lets you copy or delete documents or groups of documents and rename documents. When you choose the command, Word displays the File Management dialog box. This dialog box offers nine command buttons: Search, Summary, Options, Print, Delete, Rename, Copy, Open, and Close.

Search

To specify the criteria for a search of documents, type Alt+S for Search. Fill in the specifications that files must meet and then press Enter. Word lists the documents that meet all specifications.

Even before you fill in fields of the Search command, you can narrow your search by marking the files you want to include in a search: To mark a file, select its name and press the Spacebar. An asterisk will appear next to its name. To unmark a file, press the Spacebar again. To mark or unmark all files at once, press Ctrl+Spacebar.

Search Paths Type the name(s) of one or more directories you want Word to search, or choose them from the Directories list box. Separate directories with commas or semicolons, and use the wildcards *?* and *∗* if you like. For example, type *c:\forecast.doc* to list only a file called FORECAST.DOC in the root (top-level) directory. Type *C:\forecast* or *c:\forecast* to list all documents (with the .DOC extension) in a subdirectory called FORECAST. Type *c:\forecast\∗.fil* to list all files with the .FIL extension that are in the FORECAST subdirectory. And type *c:\forecast\,c:\plans\91* to search for documents that appear in the FORECAST subdirectory *or* the 91 subdirectory of the PLANS subdirectory.

Word remembers the last path used in a Search command, even between editing sessions, and proposes it again the next time you use File Management. To search the current directory, press Del and then press Enter.

Author Type the name(s) of one or more authors (80 characters maximum). If you list more than one, separate them with logical operators (see below).

Operator Type the name(s) of one or more operators (80 characters maximum). If you list more than one, separate them with logical operators (see below). (The Operator field refers to people who typed or worked on a document; ''logical operators'' are syntax used during a search.)

Keywords Type one or more keywords (80 characters maximum). If you list more than one, separate them with logical operators (see below).

Text If you're looking only for documents that contain specific known words or passages, type the desired text in this field (80 characters maximum).

Date Saved Specify a range of acceptable dates, using the >, <, &, and ~ logical operators explained below (25 characters maximum). For example, to search for documents created in June of 1991, type *>5/31/91&<7/1/91*. Dates must follow the format used in the Date field of the Customize dialog box (Utilities menu).

Date Created Specify a range of acceptable dates, as in the Date Saved field, explained above.

Match Case Check this box if you want Word to locate only documents that contain text that exactly matches the sequence of uppercase and lowercase letters specified in the Text field. If case doesn't matter, do not check this field.

Selected Files Only If you want to limit your search to specific files, first mark them before using the Search command, and then choose this option.

The following hints might be helpful as you use the Search command:

■ Wildcards are permitted in the following fields: Search Paths, Author, Operator, Keywords, and Text.

■ You can use the following logical operators in any field except Search Paths and Match Case:

Logical operator	Meaning
, (comma)	OR
&	AND
~ (tilde)	NOT
<	EARLIER THAN (in dates only)
>	LATER THAN (in dates only)

For example, to generate a list of all documents that contain either the letter sequence *silicon* OR the letter sequence *carbon*, you type *silicon,carbon* in the Text field. (The term *letter sequence* is used rather than *word* because in this search Word doesn't distinguish between *carbon* and *carbonate*—it looks for the six-letter sequence whether or not it's a separate word.) To generate a list of documents that contain both *silicon* AND *carbon*, type *silicon&carbon*. To generate a list of documents that contain *silicon* but NOT *carbon*, type *silicon~carbon*. To generate a list of documents that contain *car* but NOT *carbon* (or *carbonate*, for that matter), type *car~carbon*.

■ To narrow a search, you can use parentheses as punctuation. For example, to search for documents containing the word *Moon* OR both of the words *Mars* and *Saturn*, type *Moon,(Mars&Saturn)*.

- To search for text that includes one or more of the characters that represent logical operators, enclose the entire string of text in quotation marks. For example, to search for *Ways & Means*, type *"Ways & Means"*. To search for both *Ways & Means* and *Ends & Means*, type *"Ways & Means"&"Ends & Means"*.

- When the text being sought includes quotation marks, double the quotation marks and enclose the entire string in yet another set of quotation marks. To search for the phrase *"Ends justify means," he said.*, type: *"""Ends justify means,""" he said."*

- Press Esc to interrupt the Search command during a search.

Summary

To update the summary information for the document whose name is selected, press Alt+U. Now fill in or edit the summary information fields, and press Enter.

Choosing Summary also is handy when you want to read the fields of a summary sheet without setting the View Files option (see below) to *Full*.

Options

To control the order in which documents are listed and the amount of information provided about each, press Alt+T to choose the Options command button, set one or both of the following two fields, and press Enter:

Sort Files By Documents are listed in alphanumeric order, by the option you choose. For example, if you choose Author, documents are listed alphabetically by author name. If you choose Date Created, documents are listed in the order of their creation, from earliest to most recent.

View Files To see a multicolumn list of document names, including their drives and paths, choose *Short*. To see a single-column list of document names and titles, choose *Long*. To see a multicolumn list of document names and the summary sheet of the highlighted document name, choose *Full*.

Update List After Copy or Rename Check this box if you
want the list of files to be updated each time you copy or
rename a file. If you do not check this box, the list of files
might become obsolete as you use File Management commands that affect the files listed.

Print

To print the document(s) and/or summary information(s)
of either the document whose name is highlighted or all
marked documents, press Alt+P, which takes you to the
Print dialog box.

To print only summary information, choose Summary Info
in the Print drop-down list box. To print both documents
and summary information, choose Options (Alt+O) and
turn on the Summary Info check box. To print only the
document(s), turn off the Summary Info check box and be
sure to choose Document in the Print drop-down list box.

Delete

To delete a file or a group of files, first mark them, and
then choose the Delete command button in the File Management dialog box.

Rename

To rename a document, highlight it in the Files list box,
and then choose Rename. Type the new filename. (If you
want to assign a new path to the document, type it also or
choose it from the Directories list box.)

Copy

To copy a file or a group of files to a new location, mark
the desired files, and choose the Copy command button.
Then set the following fields of its dialog box as appropriate, and press Enter:

Path Name Type the name of the drive and directory to
which you want the marked documents copied, or use the
Directories list box to choose a path.

Copy Style Sheets Check this box if you also want to
move the style sheets currently attached to the document.
This ensures that not only a document's content, but its

formatting—in the form of a style sheet—is moved. Style sheets copied with a document will not be deleted, even if Delete Files After Copy is checked.

Delete Files After Copy Check this box if you want the documents to be deleted from the original drive and directory after they have been copied to the new drive and directory.

Open

To open the document whose name is selected, press Alt+O (for Open) and then press Enter. Unlike in earlier versions of Word, the document you open does not replace the active document; it is simply opened in another window.

Close

To exit the File Management dialog box and go to the text window, choose the Close button or press Esc.

See also: Directories and subdirectories; Opening a document; Path; Saving a document; Summary information; Wildcards.

Filenames and extensions

Filenames can be a maximum of eight characters, followed by a period and an extension of a maximum of three characters.

Word uses the filename extension .DOC for documents, .STY for style sheets, and .GLY for glossaries. When you load or save any of these files, you needn't type these extensions; Word appends them.

To load or save a document that has no extension, type the first part of the name and a period.

In addition, Word uses filenames with the extension .SVD, .SVG, and .SVS for autosave files, and the Capture program creates graphics images with proposed names that end with .LST and .SCR.

See also: ASCII files; Autosave; Capture; Glossary; Style sheet window.

Flush left

See: Paragraph formatting; Tabs.

Flush right

See: Paragraph formatting; Tabs.

Font names and sizes

See: Character formatting; Downloadable fonts.

Footers

See: Headers and footers.

Footnotes

To place a footnote in a document, place the cursor where you want the footnote reference mark to appear, and then choose Insert Footnote (Alt+IN). Press Enter to use the next available number (beginning with 1) as the footnote

reference mark, or type an asterisk or some other footnote
reference mark and then press Enter.

When you execute Insert Footnote, Word jumps to the end
of the document, where footnote text is stored. The reference mark appears again, and you can type footnote text
after it. When you're done, choose Edit Go To (Alt+EO) to
return to the reference mark in the body of the text.

If you delete a footnote reference mark from the main text,
the associated footnote text also is deleted. If you reinsert
the mark, the text is reinserted. If Word is numbering the
footnotes for you, it updates the numbers when you move or
delete footnote reference marks.

To control whether footnotes are printed at the bottoms of
pages or at the end of a document (or section of a document), use Format Section (Alt+TS). To open a special
window for viewing footnotes, use View Footnotes/Annota-
tions (Alt+VF). To superscript footnote reference marks
one at a time, use Format Character (Alt+TC) or the built-
in superscript character format (hold down Ctrl and Shift
and press the = key twice). The easiest way to superscript
reference marks is to create a dedicated Character Footnote
Ref style in a style sheet and format it to be superscripted
(and possibly in a smaller font). The easiest way to format
footnote paragraphs is to create a dedicated Paragraph
Footnote style in a style sheet and format it as you like
(with a smaller font, perhaps).

An annotation is a special kind of footnote.

See also: Annotations; Automatic styles; Built-in formats;
Character formatting; Section formatting; Styles;
Windows.

Formatting a document

See: Section formatting.

Formatting a paragraph

See: Paragraph formatting.

Formatting characters

See: Character formatting.

Formatting keys

See: Appendix; Built-in formats.

Form letters

See: Merging.

Forms

Word allows you to create a document and then reuse it as a form.

Creating a Form

You can turn any document into a form by adding to it one or more ''right chevron'' (») characters. To create a » character, hold down Ctrl and press the right bracket key ( ]). To prevent the » character from printing, format it as hidden text: Select (highlight) it, hold down Ctrl, and press H

(AH if a macro uses Ctrl+H). Place this hidden character at
the beginning of any blank that you might want to fill in
when filling out the form.

For example, if your form has the word *Name* followed by
an underlined blank area, place the hidden » at the beginning of the underline. Do the same for other blanks that
you'll want to fill out when you use the form. You must
create each blank with a *single* tab character and tab stop,
not with Spacebar spaces (see below). If you want, add
lines, boxes, or borders to enhance the appearance of your
form. When you are done, save this document, which we'll
call the master form.

To use the master form, first load it with File Open
(Alt+FO or Alt+Ctrl+F2). As a safeguard, turn on the dialog box's Read Only check box before you press Enter to
carry out the command. (This prevents you from accidentally overwriting the master form when you save the filled-
out version of the form.) Once the master form is loaded,
hold down Ctrl, and press the key that has the period and
the >; these actions move you to the first hidden », which is
at the beginning of the first blank to be filled in. Now hold
down Ctrl and press > again to move to the next blank. To
move to a previous blank (as marked by the hidden » character), hold down Ctrl and press the key that has the comma
and the <. Once the master form is filled out, you can print
it like any other document. If the hidden » characters print
and you don't want them to, choose File Print (Alt+FP;
Alt+O) and turn off the Hidden Text check box in the Print
Options dialog box.

To save a filled-out form, choose File Save As (Alt+FA or
Alt+F2), type a new name, and press Enter. This creates a
new document but leaves the master form intact on disk, its
blanks unfilled. Reload the master form with File Open,
and you're ready to fill it out again, in a different way.

Creating Blanks with Tabs

When creating blanks in your master form, use tabs instead
of Spacebar spaces. For example, to create a line that has
blanks for *Name* and *Phone*, start a fresh line that has no

left or first-line indent, and follow these steps. (1) Choose
Format Tabs (Alt+TT). (2) Type .5 in the Tab Position text
box, be sure the alignment is Left and the Leader is None,
and choose Set. (3) Type 4.0 in the Tab Position text box,
choose the underline option (number 4) in the Leader box,
and choose Set again. (4) Type 4.8 in the Tab Position text
box, choose the *None* option in the Leader box, and choose
Set again. (5) Type 6.0 in the Tab Position text box, choose
the underline in the Leader field, and press Enter.

Now, starting at the beginning of the line, type *Name*, press
the Spacebar, press Tab, press the Spacebar twice, type
Phone, press the Spacebar, press Tab, and press Enter. The
form should look like this:

Name ——————————————————— **Phone** —————————

If your line doesn't look like this, verify that the Spaces
check box is turned off in the View menu's Preferences
dialog box, that the Font field is *not* set to a proportional
font (if in doubt, use a ''modern a'' font such as Pica or
Courier), that the Point Size field is set to 12 with Format
menu's Character dialog box, and that the line is formatted
to be at least 60 characters wide.

Now select the first underlined blank, all of which at once
becomes highlighted because it actually is a single tab
character. Hold down Ctrl and press], which inserts a » at
the beginning of the underlined blank. Select the », hold
down Ctrl, and press H (AH if a macro code uses Ctrl+H),
making the » hidden. Use the Hidden Text check box in the
View menu's Preferences dialog box to determine whether
you see hidden text on screen. Select the second underlined
blank and repeat the steps to add a hidden » character.

Your two-field form is complete, and you can move back
and forth between its underlined blanks by using the
Ctrl+> and Ctrl+< combinations. Once you're in a blank,
you can fill it in by holding down Ctrl and pressing U (AU
if a macro code uses Ctrl+U) and then typing. Ctrl+U formats the text you're about to type as underlined so that it
matches the underline of the form. If you haven't underlined fields in your form, you needn't format what you type
as underlined.

See also: Hidden text; Lines; Merging; Tabs.

Frames

Every paragraph is surrounded by an invisible frame,
equivalent to a property line posted with "No Trespassing"
signs. The frame stakes out the region on the printed page
into which no other paragraphs can intrude. A paragraph's
contents can be text or graphics or both and needn't use all
of the real estate reserved by the frame.

By default, a paragraph's frame is as wide as a column of
normal text. To adjust the frame width, select (highlight)
the paragraph(s) and choose Format Position (Alt+TO).
Move to the Paragraph Width field and either type a number representing the desired width (generally in inches) or
press Alt+Down to see a list of common widths.

Note: *You cannot narrow the frame of a paragraph merely
by increasing its left indent and/or right indent. In this case,
the frame will remain as wide as the line length before indentation occurred. To narrow a frame, you must use the Format
Position command.*

See also: Absolute positioning.

Function keys

Word assigns a broad range of tasks to the function keys,
which are numbered F1 through F10 or F1 through F12.
How a key functions depends on whether it is pressed alone
or in combination with the Ctrl, Shift, or Alt key. For a
summary of functions, see the Appendix, or (if you have a
Help file on your disk) type Alt+HK to see Help devoted to
uses of the keyboard.

You can assign new purposes to function keys by creating a macro that performs the desired task and then assigning a function key as the macro's control code.

See also: Control codes; Macros.

Gallery

See: Style sheet window.

Glossary

The glossary is a storage area for often-used text or macros. Unlike earlier versions of Word, Word 5.5 uses separate commands to manipulate text entries and macros.

Creating and Using Text Glossary Entries

To create, manipulate, or insert a text glossary entry, choose Edit Glossary (Alt+EO). You will be taken to the Glossary dialog box, which contains eight command buttons.

Define To define text as a glossary entry, select (highlight) the text, choose Edit Glossary (Alt+EO), type a glossary name, type an optional control code in the Optional keys field, and choose Define (Alt+D). This creates a glossary entry with the name you have typed. A glossary name, including any control keys, can be a maximum of 31 characters and can't contain spaces or symbols other than an underline, a hyphen, or a period.

Insert To insert text from the glossary into a document, position the cursor where you want the text to appear, and either type the entry's name and press F3 or choose Edit Glossary, highlight the entry in the Names list box, and choose Insert (Alt+I).

Delete To delete a glossary entry, highlight its name in the Names list box and choose Delete.

Clear All To clear the glossary of all entries except the reserved glossary names, choose Clear All, and then press Enter when Word asks *Do you want to delete all glossary entries now?* Clear All clears entries from the glossary in Word's memory (RAM), but it doesn't clear the copy of the glossary that might be on disk. To do that, use Save Glossary to store the edited version of the glossary on disk.

Open Glossary Use this command to load a glossary file and replace existing glossary entries with it. Type the name of the glossary you want to load in the File Name text box, or choose it from the Files list box, and then press Enter. Turn on the Read Only check box if you want to prevent accidental changes to the glossary file.

Save Glossary Use this command to save a collection of glossary entries as a glossary file for use during later editing sessions. Macros stored in the glossary will be saved along with the text entries.

If you are saving the glossary for the first time, or if you want to give an edited glossary a new name (to preserve a previous version under the current name), type a new name in the File Name text box. You needn't type a filename extension; Word adds the extension .GLY.

If you use the name NORMAL, which Word names NORMAL.GLY, Word loads the glossary file when you start the program. This lets you create a collection of text passages and macros that are always available to you — almost as if they were built into Word.

Merge Use this command to load a glossary file and combine its contents with existing glossary entries. Type the name of the glossary whose entries you want to add, or choose it from the Files list box. Then press Enter.

Close When you are through editing your glossary entries, choose this button (or press Esc) to return to your document.

Creating and Using Macros

Although macros and text glossary entries are similar and can be stored together in the same .GLY file, Word 5.5 uses a different command—the Macro menu's Edit command—to manipulate macros.

When you choose Macro Edit (Alt+ME), you are taken to the Edit Macro dialog box. This is very similar to the Glossary dialog box and also has eight command buttons. Seven of these (Define, Delete, Clear All, Open Glossary, Save Glossary, Merge, and Close) are the same as those in the Glossary dialog box and work in the same way. Only one—Edit—is different:

Edit The Edit button is similar to the Insert button in the Glossary dialog box: It inserts the text of a glossary entry into a document. In this case, the text of the macro is inserted into your document so that you can study it, or modify it and save it in a different form.

Using Reserved Glossary Names

The following entries are permanent parts of the glossary; their names are reserved and can't be used for other glossary entries:

- *clipboard*—inserts the contents of the Windows clipboard (if you are running Word under Windows/286, Windows /386, or 386 Enhanced mode of Windows version 3)

- *date*—displays the current date on the screen and prints it

- *dateprint*—prints the date as of the time of printing

- *footnote*—restores a deleted reference mark for an automatically numbered footnote

- *nextpage*—prints the number of the following page

- *page*—prints the number of the current page

- *time*—displays the current time on the screen and prints it

- *timeprint*—prints the time of printing

To use these permanent glossary entries, either type the name and press F3 or choose Edit Glossary (Alt+EO), highlight the entry in the Names box, and choose Insert.

See also: Clipboard; Deleting a glossary entry; Deleting text; Macros; NORMAL.GLY; Printing.

Graphics, printing in a document

See: Linking graphics.

Graphics mode and text mode

See: Display mode.

Gutters

See: Section formatting.

Headers and footers

To place a header or footer (called a ''running head'' in earlier versions of Word) in a document, type the text of the header or footer and place the cursor in it. Then choose the Format menu's Header/Footer command (Alt+TH), set the following fields of the dialog box as appropriate, and press Enter:

Format as Choose Header to have the text print at the top
of pages. Choose Footer to have the text print at the bottom
of pages. Choose None to remove header/footer formatting.

(Print on) First Page Do you want the header/footer to
print on the first page of the document or section? (Headers
and footers are often omitted on title or cover pages. If you
check this box, you must make the header/footer the first
paragraph in the section.)

(Print on) Odd Pages Do you want the header/footer to
print on odd-numbered pages?

(Print on) Even Pages Do you want the header/footer to
print on even-numbered pages?

Alignment Do you want the header/footer to align with the
left margin (as established by section formatting) or with
the left edge of the paper?

If you choose Edge of Paper, use paragraph formatting to
create an appropriate left indent and right indent so that
text aligns as desired. Specifically, to have headers and
footers align with body paragraphs, use Paragraph to set
the left and right indents of the header/footer paragraph to
equal the left and right page margins. However, if you use a
right-aligned tab stop at the right margin of such a running
head, you will want to set the paragraph's right indent to 0.

For maximum ease in using headers or footers, create a
dedicated paragraph header/footer style with the indentations and tab stops you want. Then, to create the header or
footer, merely select the paragraph and use the Header/
Footer command. Word applies the style for you.

Headers and footers are not displayed in layout view. The
header or footer will print; it just isn't on the page.

See also: Automatic styles; Glossary (Using Reserved
Glossary Names); Page numbers; Section formatting
(Format Margins); Style bar.

Help

To see screens of helpful information about Word, press
Alt+HI (or press F1 when no drop-down menus, dialog
boxes, or messages are displayed) to reach the Help Index,
where you can choose among listed Help topics; or press F1
to get help that pertains to the command you're using at the
time. If you have a mouse installed, you can get Help by
clicking on the <F1=Help> button on the last line of the
screen.

The text you see when you use the Help command is deter-
mined by the Help file that is installed. Word comes with a
basic file. More extensive information is available in
MasterWord Help.

To backtrack through the Help topics you have referred to
during a Word session, choose the Back button or press
Backspace while you are in the Help window. Word keeps
track of the last 20 topics you have referred to; if you try to
go further, Word displays the message *There are no more
Help topics in the backtrack list.*

To leave the Help window and return to your document,
press Esc. To return to your document without closing the
Help window, press Ctrl+F6 or choose the document window from the bottom of the drop-down Window menu. (If
you are using MasterWord Help, you can also choose the
<5=Exit> button.)

See also: MasterWord Help; Product support.

Hidden text

To format characters as hidden, first select (highlight) the
characters and then use one of the following three methods:

Format Character

Choose Format Character (Alt+TC), turn on the Hidden
check box, and press Enter.

Built-In Format

Hold down Ctrl and press H. If a macro in your glossary
uses Ctrl+H as a control code, apply the built-in hidden
format by holding down Ctrl and pressing AH.

Styles

If a style sheet is attached to your document and if it includes a character style for hidden text, press Ctrl+Y and
type the one-character or two-character key code of the
style, such as HC (for Hidden Character). To see which
styles are available in a style sheet, choose Format Apply
Styles (Alt+TY) and choose Character in the Style Type
field, or choose Format Define Styles (Alt+TD) to look in
the style sheet window.

Comments

Often Word formats characters to be hidden, as when it includes hidden-text messages at the beginning and end of
indexes created with Insert Index or of tables of contents
created with Insert Table of Contents.

To display hidden characters in a text window, choose
View Preferences, turn on the Hidden Text check box, and
press Enter. To print hidden text, choose File Print
(Alt+FP), choose Options, and turn on the Hidden Text
check box.

See also: Built-in formats; Character formatting; Forms;
Indexing; Key codes; Linking graphics; Styles; Style sheet
window; Tables of contents; View Preferences.

Highlighting

See: Selecting text.

Hyphenating

To insert a hyphen in a document, press the hyphen (-) key.
To insert an optional hyphen, hold down Ctrl and press the
hyphen key. To insert a nonbreaking hyphen, which keeps
both halves of the word or term on the same line, hold
down Shift and Ctrl and press the hyphen key. To insert a
dash, type two consecutive nonbreaking hyphens.

In addition, you can press Ctrl+Alt+hyphen twice to insert
a dash (long hyphen) into your document. This dash appears on the screen, but prints only on certain printers, and
only after modifications are made to the printer's .PRD
file.

To have Word hyphenate the text of an entire document,
place the cursor at the top of the document and choose
Utilities Hyphenate (Alt+UH). To hyphenate a single word,
a paragraph, or any other portion of a document, select it
and then choose Utilities Hyphenate.

The hyphens the Hyphenate command adds are called "optional" or "nonrequired" because they're displayed and
printed only when they break a word at the end of a line.
(They also appear when the Optional Hyphens check box
of the View menu's Preferences dialog box is turned on.)
The command adds a hyphen between two syllables of a
multisyllabic word if the word doesn't already have a
hyphen and if the addition of the hyphen would allow one
or more syllables of the word to move up to the end of the
previous line.

You can use two fields to refine the operation of the Hyphenate command.

Confirm Turn this check box off if you want Word to hyphenate the text of the document or selection without con-
firmation. Turn it on if you want Word to ask you to
approve each hyphen. Word highlights the location where it
proposes to place a hyphen and displays a small dialog box.

Choose *Yes* in the dialog box to accept the proposed hyphenation point. To hyphenate the word at a different place, press the Left or Right direction key to move to that place, or press the Up or Down direction key to move the highlight to other points that Word recognizes as acceptable for hyphenation. Then choose *Yes*.

Choose *No* to skip the word but continue hyphenating. Press Esc to cancel further hyphenation.

Hyphenate Caps Turn this check box on if you want Word to hyphenate words that begin with a capital letter.

Note: *Hyphenation is available in French, German, Swedish, Italian, Spanish, Danish, and British English, as well as in American English. These foreign-language hyphenation routines are part of Microsoft's foreign-language spell-checking programs, sold separately.*

I.D.

See: Styles.

Indenting

See: Paragraph formatting.

Indexing

To index a document, first code the entries throughout the document and then choose Insert Index (Alt+II), which compiles and formats the index.

Coding

To designate (code) text as an index entry, type .i. immediately before the entry and ; immediately after it. If the phrase is immediately followed by a paragraph or section mark, you can omit the semicolon. Format the .i. and ; codes as hidden text.

To include words in the index entry that aren't in the document, add the words but format them as hidden text. If you want the index entry to use completely different words from those in the document, make the entire entry hidden. For example, if the document uses the word *Mikhail* but you want to index *Gorbachev*, place the cursor under the *M* of *Mikhail*, turn on hidden text by holding down Ctrl and pressing H (or Ctrl+AH), and type .i.Gorbachev;.

The simplest index has only one level of entries. Most indexes, however, have two or three levels of entries. Subentries are indented under main entries. To code a subentry, use hidden text to type a path of words or phrases leading from a main entry to the subentry. Place a colon between the main entry and the subentry. For example, you could code references to Mikhail Gorbachev with the following hidden text: .i.Gorbachev:Mikhail;, and you could code references to Raisa Gorbachev with the following hidden text: .i.Gorbachev:Raisa;. Once compiled, the index would include *Gorbachev* as a heading with *Mikhail* and *Raisa* as indented subentries under it. Each subentry would have its own list of page numbers.

Coding is much faster if you use a macro designed for the task.

Compiling

Before compiling the index, go to the File menu's Print Options dialog box (Alt+FP, then Alt+O) and turn off the Hidden Text check box.

To compile the index, choose Insert Index, set the following fields of the dialog box as appropriate, and press Enter:

Separate Page Numbers from Entry by In the compiled index, Word separates entries from page numbers with a tab character unless you specify some other separator by typing it in this field.

Capitalize Main Entries Do you want to capitalize the first word of each main (first-level) entry?

(Indent Each Level) By Word indents each subentry 0.2 inch relative to the higher-level entry preceding it unless you type a different value in this field or choose the Use Style Sheet option.

(Indent Each Level) Use Style Sheet Do you want Word to use the dedicated Index level styles in a style sheet to individually control the formatting of each level of entry? If you check this box, Word disregards the By field and formats the index according to the Index level 1, Index level 2, Index level 3, and Index level 4 styles in the style sheet. If some of these styles aren't in the style sheet or if no style sheet is attached, Word uses normal paragraph formatting for the entries.

See also: Hidden text.

Inserting tabs

See: Tabs.

Inserting text

To insert text from the scrap, press Shift+Ins or choose Edit Paste (Alt+EP).

To insert text from the glossary, position the cursor where you want the text to appear, type the name of the entry, and press F3. You can also choose Edit Glossary, highlight the desired entry in the Names list box, and press Enter.

To insert text that is bookmarked elsewhere, use Insert File.

To include one document with another when using Word's Print Merge (form letter) feature, use the INCLUDE instruction.

See also: Copying text to the scrap; Deleting text; Glossary; Linking documents; Merging; Moving text.

Insertion point

See: Cursor.

Italic characters

To format characters as italic, first select (highlight) the characters and then use one of these three methods:

Format Character
Choose Format Character (Alt+TC), turn on the Italic check box, and press Enter.

Built-In Format
Hold down Ctrl and press I. If a style sheet is attached to your document, hold down Ctrl and press AI.

Styles
If a style sheet is attached to your document and if it includes a character style for italic, press Ctrl+Y and type the one-character or two-character key code of the style, such as IC (for Italic Character). If you have a macro that uses Ctrl+Y as its control code, apply a style by typing Ctrl+AY and the key code. To see which styles are available in a style sheet, choose Format Apply Styles (Alt+TY) and choose Character in the Style Type field, or choose Format Define Styles (Alt+TD) to look in the style sheet window. If your interest is limited to paragraph styles, you can

review available choices by pressing Ctrl+S (once or twice)
to use the ribbon to view the style names.

If you want to apply the formatting *before* typing the characters, highlight a single character, apply the style, and
then type.

Comments

Although you can format characters as italic, they won't
print that way unless your printer and .PRD file can print
italic. Furthermore, they will appear on the screen as italic
only if your computer has a graphics card and if you are in
a graphics (as opposed to text) mode.

See also: Applying a style; Built-in formats; Character
formatting; Key codes; Printer files; Ribbon; Styles; Style
sheet window.

Jumping through a document

To jump to a specific page, choose Edit Go To (Alt+EG) or
press F5. Type the number of the page in the Go To text
box, choose the Page option, and press Enter. Your screen
displays the specified page if it exists.

To jump to the next footnote reference in a document or to
move between a footnote reference and the footnote text to
which it refers, choose the Footnote option of Edit Go To.

Similarly, to jump between an annotation reference mark
and the annotation text to which it refers, choose the Annotation option.

To jump to text that has been labeled with a bookmark,
choose the Bookmark option of Edit Go To, and type the
bookmark name in the Go To text box or highlight it in the
Bookmark Name list box. Then press Enter.

To jump to a particular heading in a document, use Word's
outlining feature.

To jump to a particular region in a document, use the mouse to drag the scroll box down the vertical scroll bar (point to the scroll box, press the left mouse button, drag, and release), about as far as you want to jump in the document. In other words, to jump to the beginning of the document, drag the scroll box to the top of the scroll bar; to jump to the middle of the document, drag the scroll box to a point halfway down the scroll bar.

See also: Annotations; Bookmarks; Footnotes; Mouse; Outlining; Repaginating.

Justifying

See: Paragraph formatting.

Key codes

A key code consists of one or two characters that identify a particular style from a style sheet. To use a key code to format text with a style, select (highlight) the text, press Ctrl+Y, and type the code.

Designate a key code when you create a style with either Format Record Style (Alt+TR) or the style sheet window's Insert New Style command. You can change a key code with the style sheet window's Edit Rename Style command.

Although a key code can consist of one character, two characters are preferable because they allow for a greater number of combinations.

Note: *A key code applies a style from a style sheet; a control code runs a macro or inserts a text entry from the glossary.*

See also: Applying a style; Automatic styles; Built-in formats; Control codes; Recording a style; Styles; Style sheets; Style sheet window.

Layout techniques

The layout powers of Word 5.5 come from the interaction of several commands:

- Format Section controls the number of columns on the page and changes in the numbers of columns.

- Format Margins controls the page size and margins.

- Format Paragraph controls the left and right indents as well as the space before and after paragraphs.

- Insert Picture imports and controls the size of graphics created outside of Word so that Word treats them as paragraphs.

- Format Position fixes text or graphics paragraphs to particular places on the page and controls the width of those paragraphs.

- Format Borders puts boxes or shaded boxes around one or more paragraphs. (Or use the Utilities Line Draw command.)

See also: Absolute positioning; Lines; Linking graphics; Paragraph formatting; Section formatting.

Layout view

To see and work with an on-screen approximation of page layout, choose View Layout (Alt+VL). The letters LY appear on the last line of the screen, indicating that you are in layout view.

In this view of your document, multiple columns, side-by-side paragraphs, and graphics elements appear in the approximate locations where they will print. The display isn't perfect (every character has the same width, and graphics appear as boxes), but layout view, unlike print preview mode, does allow editing. (Print preview provides a more accurate representation of what will print but prohibits editing.) Layout view can be highly useful, yet challenging: In layout view the rules of navigating around the document change because in a sense you can see and work on a number of different elements (such as columns or boxed paragraphs) at once. On all but the fastest computers, lags can occur while Word races to perform the heavy load of calculations required to keep the screen up to date as you make editing changes.

If you enter layout view in a blank window, a paragraph mark appears. Ignore it; you cannot delete it.

To move between columns or other side-by-side elements, first hold down Alt and press the 5 key. Then press either the Left or Right direction key, depending on which way you want to move. After you are within an object (such as a column), press Ctrl+Up to jump to its first character or Ctrl+Down to jump to its last character.

In layout view, the ruler (if displayed) is reduced in length to span only the top of the current column (or paragraph). This lets tab stops be displayed relative to the paragraphs to which they relate.

In layout view, revision marks appear on screen only for the leftmost column, although they print for all columns.

Headers and footers are not displayed in layout view.

Display of hidden text is controlled by the Hidden Text check box of the File menu's Print Options dialog box.

See also: Columns, multiple; Headers and footers; Previewing printing; Revision marks; Ruler; Side-by-side text.

Left-alignment

See: Paragraph formatting; Tabs.

Legal documents

See: Line numbers.

Level

See: Outlining.

Line breaks

See: New line.

Line numbers

To print line numbers in the left margin of a document, choose Format Section (Alt+TS) and turn on the Add Line Numbers check box. These numbers appear on the screen only in print preview mode.

To display line numbers in the lower-left corner of the screen, choose View Preferences (Alt+VE) and turn on the Show Line Numbers check box. If you want Word to count as lines those blank lines that are created through formatting (such as paragraph space after and space before), turn on the Count Blank Space check box. Displaying line numbers slows Word significantly for some tasks.

See also: Section formatting; View Preferences.

Lines

To draw horizontal and vertical lines in a document, choose Utilities Line Draw (Alt+UL) to turn on the linedraw mode and then use the direction keys to lay down the lines. You can also use the direction keys to move back over a line without erasing it. To turn off the linedraw mode, press Esc.

You can undo your recent line drawing with Edit Undo (Alt+EU or Alt+Backspace), but you'll lose your place in the document because Word selects (highlights) the entire document after undoing line drawing. You can erase a horizontal line by turning off the linedraw mode and using the Backspace key.

To determine which of 12 special characters Word uses to draw straight lines, choose Utilities Customize (Alt+UU), move to the Line Draw Character field of the dialog box, use the direction keys to scroll through the list of options, and press Enter when the desired option is highlighted. You can also use as a linedraw character any character on the keyboard or any characters from the extended character set (use the Alt+number code key combination)—just type it into the Line Draw Character field.

If you're using a proportional font in your document, don't attempt to draw lines with this method.

If your printer and .PRD file do not support the extended character set, printed lines are drawn with the bar/hyphen set.

If you us   le sheet and it has a Character Line draw
style, Wo   l use this style (and the font specified in this
style) to   t the lines you draw.

To draw   rs or lines around paragraphs, you can use
the Form   nu's Borders command (Alt+TB). To draw
horizont   s in tables, use the Format menu's Tabs command (A   ') and choose the underline (_) in the Leader
field. To   vertical lines in a table, use Format Tabs
(Alt+T'   set the Alignment field to *Vertical*.

See also: Automatic styles; Paragraph formatting (Format
Borders); Tabs; Utilities Customize.

Line spacing

See: Paragraph formatting.

Linking documents

To link one document with another document, or with a
bookmarked section of another document, choose Insert
File (Alt+IF), set the following fields of the dialog box as
appropriate, and press Enter. (If you want to import only a
portion of the document, the portion must be marked and
named in advance, using Insert Bookmark.)

File Name Type the name of the document you want to
fully or partially incorporate, or choose its name from the
Files list box. If the desired document is not in the current
directory, precede its name with a drive letter and directory, as necessary, or choose a directory from the Directories list box.

Range To insert all of the document, choose All. To incorporate only a marked portion of the document named
in the previous field, type the name of the bookmarked

passage here, or press Alt+Down to choose from a list of
bookmark names.

Word inserts the specified document or bookmarked text
(preceded and followed by the character .D. in hidden text)
at the location of the cursor. Following the first .D., also in
hidden text, are the drive, path, and name of the imported
document and the name of the bookmark (if any).

See also: Bookmarks; Hidden text; Linking graphics;
Linking spreadsheets.

Linking graphics

Import a graphics image into Word by choosing Insert Picture, filling in the dialog box as appropriate, and pressing
Enter. The command, in turn, inserts into your document
hidden-text coding that causes Word to print the graphics
image, provided that the image is stored as a separate file
and is in one of the formats that Word understands. The
coding begins with the characters .G. and contains information from several of the following dialog box fields:

Picture File Name Type the full name of the graphics file
you want to import, or choose it from the Files list box. If
you are running Word as an application under Microsoft
Windows/286, Windows/386, or the 386 Enhanced mode
of Windows version 3, you can incorporate an image stored
in the Windows clipboard by typing *clipboard* or choosing
it from the list.

Format Word fills in this text box if it recognizes the format of the graphics file you specified in the Picture File
Name text box. Word recognizes and handles the following
formats:

■ *PCX* for bit-mapped picture files generated by many
   painting and other programs, including PC Paintbrush,
   Windows Paintbrush, HP Graphics Gallery, HP Scanning Gallery, Harvard Graphics, and the software

accompanying many scanners (including the Dest PC
Scan, HP ScanJet, Microtek MSF-300, Panasonic FX-RS
505, and Taxan Crystal Scan scanners).

■ *PCC* for bit-mapped picture files that are cropped
   portions of pictures generated by PC Paintbrush and
   Microsoft Paintbrush.

■ *PIC* for Lotus PIC graphics files.

■ *TIFF* for bit-mapped graphics files produced by many
   scanners. Word can use compressed and uncompressed
   TIFF B (black-and-white) files and uncompressed TIFF
   G (gray-scale) files. TIFF stands for Tagged Image File
   Format. Scanners that create TIFF files include the
   Canon IX 12, HP ScanJet, IBM PageScanner, Microtek
   MSF-300, Panasonic FX-RS 505, Princeton LS-300, and
   Taxan Crystal Scan. Graphics packages that produce
   TIFF files include Energraphics, HP Graphics Gallery,
   and HP Scanning Gallery.

■ *Clipboard* for bit-mapped images from the Microsoft
   Windows clipboard, including images generated by
   Microsoft Excel and Microsoft Paintbrush. (Not available with Windows 3 running in real or standard
   modes.)

■ *Screen capture* for files captured from the screen with
   the CAPTURE.COM program included with Word (beginning with version 5.0).

In addition, there are three formats Word can use but
doesn't recognize. If the file has one of the following formats, type its name in the Format field or press Alt+Down
to choose the name from a list.

■ *HPGL* for Hewlett-Packard plotter files. Graphics packages that can produce HPGL files include AutoCAD,
   ChartMaster, Energraphics, Graph-in-the-box, Graph-
   writer, Harvard Graphics, HP Graphics Gallery,
   Microsoft Chart, and Microsoft Paint.

■ *PostScript* for PostScript files that have been printed to
   a disk.

- *print file* for output that normally would go to a printer but was instead stored as ("printed to") a file.

Align in frame If the graphic is narrower than the invisible paragraph frame surrounding it, how should the graphic be aligned inside the frame? To the left? To the right? Centered? Type a distance in inches from the left side or press Alt+Down to see a list of possibilities.

Width Word proposes that the graphic be as wide as the paragraph frame, but you can type a different width (in inches, for instance). Or press Alt+Down for a list of proposed widths, including the graphic's "natural size."

Height Word proposes a proportionally correct height for the graphic, but you can specify a height (in inches, for instance) or choose from a list.

Before How much extra space do you want above the graphic? Type the number of lines to add, or type a number and a unit of measure (such as *.8"*).

After How much extra space do you want below the graphic? Type the number of lines to add, or type a number and a unit of measure (such as *.8"*).

Both the Before and After text boxes put space between the graphic and the paragraph frame. That is, the space is inside the frame. To add space between the frame and the surrounding text (that is, outside the frame) use Format Position's Distance from Text field.

Note: *MasterWord includes a utility program, FULLCOPY, that lets you copy a Word document, and all files linked to the document, to a new disk or directory. For example, if a document contains three graphics images and you use FULLCOPY to copy the document to the A drive, the three graphics files will be copied automatically, too. FULLCOPY then updates the document's content to reflect the new location of the graphics files.*

See also: Absolute positioning; Bookmarks; Capture; Clipboard; Layout techniques; Linking documents.

Linking spreadsheets

To incorporate words or numbers from a spreadsheet into a
Word document, choose Insert File (Alt+IF). The data you
import into Word can be a single cell, any rectangular
group of cells or named area, or an entire spreadsheet from
Lotus 1-2-3, Microsoft Excel, Microsoft Multiplan, or
Microsoft Works.

First, load the spreadsheet into your spreadsheet program
and identify the part you want to use. If the cell or range of
cells has a name, note it. If it doesn't have a name, give it
one using Lotus 1-2-3's Range Name Create command,
Microsoft Excel's Formula Define Name command,
Multiplan's Name command, or Works' Edit Name command. If it's a single cell and you don't want to assign it a
name, write down its address—such as *R2C1* for Multiplan
or *A2* for any of the other spreadsheet programs. You express the address for a range of cells by noting the upper-
left and lower-right corners of the rectangle, such as
R2C1:R8C5 for Multiplan or *A2..E8* for the other three
programs.

Start Word and place the cursor where you want the
spreadsheet data to appear. Choose Insert File, set the following fields of the dialog box as appropriate, and press
Enter:

File Name Type the name of the spreadsheet file from
which you are extracting data. Include the drive and path if
the spreadsheet isn't in the current directory. For example,
if your spreadsheet is called SALES.WK1 and is stored in
the \123 subdirectory of the C drive, type *c:\123\sales.wk1*.

Range From what area of the spreadsheet do you want to
extract data? Press Alt+Down to see a list of named areas,
or type the address of the cell (for example, *A2* or *R2C1*) or
a range of cells (for example, *A2-E8* or *R2C1:R8C5*).

When Word imports more than one column, it separates the
columns with a tab character. When it imports more than

one line, it separates the lines with a new-line character. Sometimes you might need to adjust the appearance of a table to get it exactly right.

Imported data is both preceded and followed by hidden text, which begins *.L.* and stores information from the fields of Insert File. Therefore, you don't have to fill the fields in again later if you update the spreadsheet and want to use the command to update the document accordingly.

To update data in the Word document to reflect changes in the spreadsheet, first select both the data and the hidden text before and after it. To update all links in the document, hold down Shift and press F10 to select the entire document. Then choose Insert File and choose Update Link, or simply press F9. Word highlights each link in turn, making the hidden text temporarily visible if it isn't already and displaying the message *Do you want to update this link? Choose yes to update or no to go on.*

Note: *The FULLCAPS utility, described under "Linking graphics," also copies spreadsheet files when they are linked to a document that is copied.*

See also: Directories and subdirectories; Linking documents; Linking graphics.

List box

A list box, one of the elements found in many dialog boxes, lets you make a choice from among known alternatives.

See also: Dialog box.

Loading a document

See: Opening a document.

Lotus 1-2-3

See: Linking spreadsheets.

Macros

Macros, which are stored in the glossary, are sequences of keystrokes that can be played back later. Optionally, you can include instructions (programming) so that macro performance depends on circumstances. Either way, a macro is a little computer program, a small script that Word follows to accomplish a task.

To use a macro, follow one of three methods:

- Hold down Shift+Ctrl and type the macro's control code. This assumes the macro has a control code that begins with Shift+Ctrl. If the control code begins with just Ctrl, then you press Ctrl plus the code. (It is recommended that you use Shift+Ctrl, for reasons explained below.)

- Type the macro's name and press F3.

- Choose Macro Run (Alt+MR), select (highlight) the desired entry in the list box, and press Enter.

Creating a Macro

To create a macro, you copy it to the glossary in either of two ways: by recording it or by writing it. Part of the creation process is to give the macro a name and an optional control code (so that you can run the macro later at the touch of a couple of keys). You also can edit macros and save them on disk for future use.

Recording a macro Turn on the macro recorder by choosing Macro Record (Alt+MC or Ctrl+F3). Type a name for the macro in the Macro Name text box. Move to

the Macro Keys field to assign a key code for the macro.
Macro key codes generally begin with Ctrl or Shift+Ctrl.
Shift+Ctrl is preferable because it prevents macro control
codes from conflicting with 23 other uses of the Ctrl key.
To assign a two-letter key code, hold down the Shift and
Ctrl keys and type the first letter, and then release Shift
and Ctrl to type the second letter. Press Enter to begin
recording the macro.

Type any series of keystrokes, including text or commands,
that you want to store. (You cannot store mouse actions in a
macro.) Now choose Macro Stop Recorder (Alt+MC or
Ctrl+F3) to turn off the record macro mode. Your keystrokes are now stored in the glossary as a macro.

Writing a macro Write a macro as if it were text, using
the macro language. You can include programming instructions when you write a macro. When finished, select the
macro text and choose Macro Edit (Alt+ME). Type a name
in the Macro Name text box and a control code in the
Macro Keys text box, and then choose Define (Alt+D).

Editing and saving a macro After a macro is stored in the
glossary, you can read and edit it in text form by inserting
it into a document. To do this, choose Macro Edit
(Alt+ME), select the desired macro name from the Macros
list box, and choose Edit (Alt+E). To store the macro after
editing it, select the text of the macro, choose Macro Edit
again, select the macro's name from the list, and choose
Define (Alt+D). Choose *OK* when Word asks *Do you want
to replace the existing macro?*

If a macro fails to perform as you expected, turn on the
Step check box in the dialog box of the Macro Run command. In step mode, Word executes one macro instruction
at a time, each time you press the Spacebar. After you
locate the problem, turn off the Step check box of the
Macro Run command, or press Esc while the macro is running and turn off the Step Mode check box in the resulting
dialog box. (Another use for step mode is to control the
speed at which a macro executes. As long as you hold down
the Spacebar, the macro races forward; as soon as you
release the Spacebar, the macro pauses.)

To save a macro or collection of macros on disk for use
during a future editing session, choose Save Glossary in the
Edit Macro dialog box.

The Macro Language

A recorded macro consists only of *keystrokes* that are stored
for playback. The language in which such a macro is composed is limited to the names of keys.

However, a macro that has been written or edited can also
include *constants, variables, array variables, reserved variables, operators, functions,* and *instructions.* Many of these
require the use of chevrons:

■ To create a left chevron («), hold down Ctrl and type a
  left bracket ([).

■ To create a right chevron (»), hold down Ctrl and type
  the right bracket (]).

Here is a rundown on each element of the macro language,
beginning with keystrokes.

Keystrokes When viewing, writing, or editing a macro,
you express letter and number keys by their own names.
You express other keys with the following names, which
are bracketed inside less-than (<) and greater-than (>)
signs. For example, you express the Enter key as <enter>,
and you express Shift+Ctrl+P as <shift ctrl P>.

Here is a list of keys and their names. When a key is to
be pressed more than once, include the number of times
inside the brackets. For instance, instead of typing
<tab><tab><tab>, you can type *<tab 3>*.

Key	Name
Alt	<alt>
Control	<ctrl>
Shift	<shift>
Escape	<esc>
Enter	<enter>
Tab	<tab>
Delete	<del>
Insert	<ins>

Key	Name
Home	<home>
End	<end>
Left	<left>
Right	<right>
Down	<down>
Up	<up>
Pagedown	<pgdn>
Pageup	<pgup>
∗ on numeric keypad	<keypad∗>
+ on numeric keypad	<keypad+>
− on numeric keypad	<keypad−>
Spacebar	<space>
Backspace	<backspace>
Num Lock	<numlock>
Scroll Lock	<scrolllock>
Caps Lock	<capslock>
F1 through F12	<f1> through <f12>

In addition, <menu> signals that the menu is to be activated or deactivated. It is an alternative to <alt> or <f10>, both of which do the same thing. Similarly, <ctrl esc> activates the menu bar even if you are in a dialog box, which it closes. It activates either the main menu bar or the print preview menu bar, which is displayed only when File Print Preview is in use. A variation is <shift ctrl esc>, which forces Word to go to the main menu regardless of whether File Print Preview is in use. It does not, however, distinguish between the main menu displayed when a document is active and the version of the main menu displayed when a style sheet is active.

Three characters are considered special by macros and must be paired with a preceding caret when they are representing themselves. The characters are the left angle bracket (<), the left chevron («), and the caret (^). In other words, you can use the left angle bracket as part of a keystroke (such as <alt>) but if you want to search for a left angle bracket you must express it as ''^<''. Similarly, you can use the left chevron as part of a macro instruction (such as «ENDIF»), but when a left chevron is representing itself it must be expressed as "^«". And when a caret is representing itself, it must be preceded by a caret: "^^".

Constants A constant is an unchanging value. Numbers, text and numbers enclosed in quotation marks, and dates are constants. Examples of constants: *98.6*, *"artist"*, *"-17.8"*, and *8/4/91*.

Constants can also include the special caret (^) characters used with Edit Search and Edit Replace, but the carets must be doubled.

Character	Description
^^?	Question mark
^^-	Nonrequired (optional) hyphen
^^c	New-column character
^^n	New-line character
^^d	Section mark or new-page mark
^^p	Paragraph mark
^^s	Nonbreaking spaces (Shift+Ctrl+Spacebar)
^^t	Tab characters
^^w	All spaces and spacing characters (including tab characters and paragraph marks)

Variables A variable can assume one or more values during the running of a macro. A variable is represented by a name, which can be any letter or word except for several reserved names. (*See:* Reserved Variables.) For example, *x* can be a variable name, as can the words *file* and *setting*. However, variable names cannot contain a period, an underscore, or a hyphen.

Array variables When you need to use a series of related variables, and particularly when the number needed might change each time you run the macro, use an array variable. Each array variable has two components: an *array name*, which you make up and which is the same for each variable in the series, and an *index number*, which is unique for each variable in the series. The index number is enclosed in chevrons (« »).

For example, a macro that adds up a store's sales each month might use an array name of *sales* and use different index numbers for each day of the month. That is, the first day's sales might be assigned the variable name *sales«1»*, the second day's *sales«2»*, and so on. The exact number of variables created would depend on the number of days in the month.

Word can accommodate a combined total of at most 64 variables, of all types, in one macro.

Reserved variables Certain names that have special purposes are set aside as *reserved variables*.

The first eight reserved variables are *read-only*, which means that you can check on or otherwise use their values in a macro but you cannot control their values with a SET instruction.

- *Field* refers to whatever is highlighted when a command field is displayed.

- *Page* refers to the current page number of the active document.

- *DialogTitle* refers to the title of a dialog box. Equals " " when a dialog box is not displayed.

- *Selection* refers to whatever is highlighted on the screen.

- *WordVersion* refers to the version of Word that is running, provided the version is 5.0 or higher. If you write a macro that will work only with version 5.5, you can begin the macro with the following instruction: *«IF Wordversion <> "5.5"»«QUIT»«ENDIF»*.

- *StartupDir* refers to the name of the directory that was active when the current Word session began.

- *ProgramDir* refers to the name of the directory in which the Word program (WORD.EXE) is stored.

- *CurrentDir* refers to the name of the current directory.

The following seven reserved variables are of both the *read-only* and *Boolean* types. A Boolean variable has a value of either true or false and does not use an operator (such as =) because the equal sign is implied. For example,

an IF statement using the reserved variable *Maximized*
would not follow the form *«IF Maximized = "true"»*
(...macro steps here...) «ENDIF», but would instead follow
the form *«IF Maximized» (...macro steps here...) «ENDIF»*.

■ *Found* is true if the last search conducted with Edit
  Search found the desired text. For example, to instruct a
  macro to delete specific text if a search for it was suc-
  cessful, you could include the following line after the
  Edit Search command: *«IF Found»<del>«ENDIF»*.

■ *Notfound* is true if the last search conducted with the
  Edit Search command failed to find the desired text.

■ *Save* is true when the SAVE indicator (on the screen's
  last line) is turned on or flashing. To have a macro save
  your document if the SAVE indicator appears while the
  macro is running, include the following statement one or
  more times: *«IF Save»<alt shift f2>«ENDIF»*.

■ *Maximized* is true when more than one window is open
  and windows are maximized. To make sure Word is
  maximized, you can include the instruction *«IF NOT
  Maximized»<Ctrl+F10> «ENDIF»*.

■ *Checked* is true when a given command (View Layout,
  for example) has a dot beside it.

■ *Help* is true when the Help window is displayed.

■ *Endmark* is true when the cursor is on the endmark (the
  small diamond that marks the end of a document). To
  stop a macro when it reaches the end of a document, you
  can include the following instruction:
  «IF Endmark»«QUIT»«ENDIF».

The final six reserved variables are *read-write*, which
means that in addition to being able to read and use their
values, you can use the SET instruction to directly change
their values.

■ *Echo* reflects whether the screen will be updated continuously as the macro executes (''on'') or whether the
  screen will not change until the macro completes its
  work (''off''). To speed up the execution of many

macros, use the instruction *«SET Echo = "off"»*. You can turn updating on and off repeatedly during a macro.

■ *Promptmode* reflects in which of three ways prompts are handled. (''Prompts'' are messages normally requiring an answer, such as *Do you want to continue searching from the beginning of the document?*) Word's default is *Macro*, in which Word expects the macro itself to supply any responses to prompts. Alternatively, you can include the instruction *«SET Promptmode = "ignore"»* if you want Word to make its own choice about how to reply to a prompt, or include the instruction *«SET Promptmode = "user"»* if you want the macro to pause so that you (or whoever is using the macro) can make a decision at the keyboard.

■ *Window* refers to the number of the active window, from 1 through 9 (or 1 through 10 if the Help window is open). You can move directly to a desired window by using the SET command. (*«SET Window = 1»* moves you to the first window, for example.)

■ *Word5Keys* allows you to turn Word 5.5's emulation of Word 5.0's function keys on or off. The instruction *«SET Word5Keys = "off"»* will force Word to use the Word 5.5 function-key assignments, even if the Use Word 5.0 Function Keys check box of the Utilities Customize command is turned on.

■ *InsOvertype* is similar to the *Word5Keys* reserved variable. Use the instruction *«SET InsOvertype = "on"»* to force Word to use the default Word 5.5 assignments for the Ins and Del keys, rather than the Word 5.0 emulation.

■ *Scrap* refers to the contents of the scrap.

Operators The following six *comparison operators* let you use IF and WHILE instructions to compare two expressions. An expression can be a constant, a variable of any kind, or a combination of constants and variables.

Operator	Description
=	Equal to
<>	Not equal to
<	Less than
<=	Less than or equal to
>	Greater than
>=	Greater than or equal to

The following *math operators* let calculations take place inside a macro:

Operator	Description
+	Add
–	Subtract
*	Multiply
/	Divide
%	Percentage
(	Open parenthesis
)	Close parenthesis

Mathematical expressions can use numbers as well as variables that represent numbers. When several calculations are included in a single SET or other instruction, calculations inside parentheses are performed before those outside parentheses.

Three additional operators are called *logical operators* because they let you refine Word's logic when it reads macro instructions.

Operator	Description
AND	Logical and (both must be true)
OR	Logical or (either must be true)
NOT	Logical not (true if the condition is false)

For example, the instruction *«IF response = "Y" OR response = "Yes"»... other macro steps here...«ENDIF»* causes the other macro steps to be executed if the variable *response* is either "Y" or "Yes."

Functions Four functions let you examine and use the values of variables:

- INT rounds a number to the next-lower whole number (or "integer"). The number can be a constant or variable, positive or negative, or a math expression. Use the form *INT(number to be rounded down)*. For example, the instruction *«SET due = INT(total)»* rounds the value of "total" down to the next-lower integer and assigns the name "due" to the value.

- LEN calculates the length of a text string. Use the form *LEN(name of variable whose length is to be measured)*. For example, the instruction *«IF LEN(Selection) > 1»* *«QUIT»«ENDIF»* causes the macro to quit if the length of the selection (the highlight on the screen) is greater than one character.

- MID lets you examine an isolated portion of a text string. Use the form *MID(string,x,y)*, where *string* is the constant or variable name of the text string the macro is to examine, *x* is the number of the first character of the string that is of interest, and *y* is how many successive characters are of interest. For example, if the variable named *car* has the value *Buick!*, the instruction *«SET choice = MID(car,3,4)»* would cause the variable named *choice* to be set to *ick!* because *car* is composed of *B,u,i,c,k,* and *!,* and because the *3* indicates that the third character is the first one of interest, and the *4* indicates the total number of characters.

- Concatenation lets you combine two or more text strings to create a new string. Unlike the other functions, there is no three-letter name for this feature. Simply place the variable names one after the other, to the right of the equal sign of a SET statement, and Word will concatenate them. For example, if the variable name *first* is set to *Mister* and the variable name *second* is set to *Ed*, then the instruction *«SET hoof = first " " second»* causes the variable name *hoof* to be set to *Mister Ed*. (If the instruction were *«SET hoof = first second»*, the variable name would be set to *MisterEd*.)

Instructions An instruction performs a specific task when Word encounters it during the running of a macro. Each instruction must be enclosed in chevrons.

The list below gives the nine macro instructions: ASK,
COMMENT, IF, MESSAGE, PAUSE, REPEAT, QUIT,
SET, and WHILE. In each case the syntax of the instruction is followed by a brief explanation and an example. Instructions are uppercase; optional elements are in square
brackets.

☐ «ASK *variable* =?*prompt*»

Asks you to type a response; assigns the response to
variable. For example:

«ASK file = ?Which file do you want to load?»

☐ «COMMENT *text*»
«COMMENT» *text* «ENDCOMMENT»

Provides explanatory text that doesn't affect the operation of the macro. For example:

«COMMENT This is an explanation.»

☐ «IF *condition*»*result*
[«ELSE»*alternate result*]«ENDIF»

Executes *result* if *condition* (containing an operator) is
true. Optionally, if *condition* is false, executes *alternate
result*. For example:

«IF file =
"PAYMENTS.DOC"»<esc>ts<enter>«ENDIF»

☐ «MESSAGE *text*»

Displays as many as 80 characters of text on the message line. For example:

«MESSAGE The macro is running.»

☐ «PAUSE [*text*]»

Waits until you press Enter, giving you an opportunity
to respond to the optional message. For example:

«PAUSE»

☐ «REPEAT *x*» *macro steps* «ENDREPEAT»

Repeats part of the macro (*macro steps*) *x* times. For
example:

«REPEAT 12»<down><enter>«ENDREPEAT»

☐ «QUIT»

Halts the macro but doesn't exit Word. Takes only one
form:

«QUIT»

☐ «SET `variable` = `expression`»
Sets *variable* equal to *expression*, where *expression* can
be a constant, a string of text in quotation marks, or a
combination of constants and variables or reserved variables. (SET can also be used in the same way as ASK.)
For example:
«SET n = n+1»

☐ «WHILE `condition`»`task(s)`«ENDWHILE»
While *condition* (containing an operator) is true, per-
forms *task(s)*. For example:
«WHILE x<10»<down>
«SET x = x+1»«ENDWHILE»

Note: *The terms in Word's macro language are not case sensitive. However, it is easier to read and understand a macro if
you follow certain conventions of capitalization. For instance,
capitalize all letters in instructions, the first letters of reserved
variables, and no letters in the names of keys.*

A Sample Macro

The following macro causes Word to switch to a different
window of your choice. Although relatively unsophisticated
in its control of windows, this macro is useful in its own
right—and as an example of the elements of a Word 5.0
macro. (Try to figure out what this macro does before you
type it in and actually run it.)

```
«SET initial = window»
«ASK query = ?You want to move to which window?»
«SET newWin = INT(query)»
«IF newWin < 1 OR newWin > 9»
     «ASK msg = ?Moving to window «newWin» is
impossible. (Press Enter.)»
     «QUIT»
«ENDIF»
«SET Window = newWin»
«IF Window <> newWin»
     «ASK msg = ?You have no window «newWin».
(Press Enter.)»
     «SET Window = initial»
     «QUIT»
«ENDIF»
```

Don't worry about the indentation of the lines following the IF statements; they are created by tab characters and have no effect on the way the macro runs (but they do make it easier to trace visually what the macro does).

The first four lines of the macro include examples of many elements of the macro language:

Example	Element
«SET...»	Instruction
initial	Variable
=	Operator
window	Reserved variable
«ASK...»	Instruction
INT( )	Function
«IF...»	Instruction (conditional type)
<	Operator
1	Constant
OR	Logical operator
9	Constant

One element the sample macro does not have is keystrokes; a macro can type text into a document, or run commands, just as if you were pressing the keys.

See also: Control codes; Deleting a glossary entry; Glossary.

Mailmerge

See: Merging.

MAKE.PRD

See: Paragraph formatting (Format Borders); Printer files.

Margins

See: Section formatting.

MasterWord Help

MasterWord Help is a comprehensive replacement for the help file that comes with Word. It is one of the files of *MasterWord,* a collection of utilities, macros, and style sheets for use with Word 5.5. (Most features work with Word 5.0 too.) You can install different components of MasterWord Help, depending on how much of your hard disk you want dedicated to on-line assistance. If all topics are installed, the help file uses approximately 1.4 MB of disk space (for its 3 million characters of information).

In addition to providing help with Word (and with such associated topics as library research and document formatting) MasterWord Help includes ACT buttons. These buttons carry out tasks for you. When you don't want to figure out exactly how to accomplish something, or you don't want to do the steps yourself, look in MasterWord Help for an ACT button that describes what you have in mind; press it and MasterWord carries out the task. To order Master-Word, contact Alki Software at 1-800-669-WORD.

See also: Help.

Math

To add, subtract, multiply, or divide numbers on the screen, insert operators between them, select (highlight) the entire expression, and press F2. (To highlight a column of numbers you want to add, first turn on the column-select mode

by holding down the Shift and Ctrl keys and pressing F8.)
Word calculates the result and places it in the scrap. To insert this result in the document, use Edit Paste (Alt+EP).

Word recognizes the following operators:

+ (or no operator)	Add
– (or parentheses around a number)	Subtract
*	Multiply
/	Divide
%	Percent

Place operators before the numbers to which they pertain,
except for %, which you should place after.

If you don't include an operator, Word assumes a + and
adds the numbers. For example, if you select a column of
numbers that have no operators and press F2, Word adds
the numbers.

If a selected expression contains several operations, Word
first calculates percentages, then it multiplies and divides,
and finally it adds and subtracts. To alter this order, use
parentheses to enclose the calculations to be performed
first—for example, *3*2+1* equals 7, but *3*(2+1)* equals 9.

If the numbers in the expression are integers, the result
contains a maximum of two decimal places. For example,
the result of *10/3* is 3.33. However, if one or more of the
numbers contain decimals, the result contains the same
number of decimals (with a maximum of 13). For example,
the result of *10.0000/3* is 3.3333.

MasterWord includes a macro that calls MasterWord Calc,
a program that performs sophisticated calculations, such as
statistical and financial functions, and inserts the results
into your Word document.

See also: Scrap; Selecting a column.

Measurements

See: Utilities Customize.

Merging

To print a series of documents that have some text in common and some text that varies, first create both a main document and a data document. Load the main document and choose File Print Merge (Alt+FM). Word prints as many merge documents, all based on the main document, as there are records in the data document.

The main document contains named blanks, called *fields*. For each merge document to be printed, Word fills in these fields with information from a line (paragraph) from the data document. Each line (paragraph) is a record and has its information organized as a series of fields separated by commas (or by semicolons, if the Decimal field of the Utilities Customize command is set to the comma). If you dedicate one record of the data document to each intended recipient of a form letter, Word creates the individual letters for you.

Preparing the Main Document

Type and save the main document as you would any other. However, include within the document guidance to Word on what variable information to incorporate during printing. Enclose in chevrons each reference to variable information, whether a field name or a merge instruction. To create a left chevron («), hold down Ctrl and type a left bracket ([); to create a right chevron (»), hold down Ctrl and type a right bracket (]). For example, in the following sentence from a main document, *«name»* is a blank Word fills in with whatever is stored in a data document's *name* field.

```
We regret to announce, «name», that Spencer
   Ceramics has declared bankruptcy.
```

Each merge instruction performs a specific task when
Word encounters it during merge printing. The following
list gives the seven merge instructions that you can include
in a main document: DATA, SET, ASK, IF, SKIP, NEXT,
and INCLUDE. In each case the syntax of the instruction
is followed by a brief explanation and an example. Instructions are uppercase; optional elements are in square
brackets.

☐ «DATA *filename*»
   Tells Word the name of the data document. Must be the
   first line in the main document. For example:
   «DATA maillist.doc»

☐ «SET *variable* = ?[*prompt*]»
   Asks you to type a response; assigns the response to
   variable for the entire series of merge documents. For
   example:
   «SET grade = ?Which grade of meat?»

☐ «ASK *variable* = ?[*prompt*]»
   Identical to SET, except that your response is used for
   only one merge document. For example:
   «ASK grade = ?Which grade of meat?»

☐ «IF *condition*»*result*[«ELSE» *alternate result*]
   «ENDIF»
   Prints *result* if *condition* (containing an operator) is true.
   Optionally, if *condition* is false, prints *alternate result*.
   Operators are =, <>, <, >, <=, and >=. (For more on
   operators, see *Macros*.) For example:
   «IF grade="choice"»You'll enjoy our choice
   meat.«ELSE»You're bound to enjoy our quality
   meats.«ENDIF»

☐ «SKIP»
   Skips the current record in the data document and restarts the merge process with the next record. For example, to cause Word not to print a merge document
   when *age* is less than 35:
   «IF age<35»«SKIP»«ENDIF»

☐ «NEXT»

Skips to the next record in the data document, but continues to produce the current merge document. Permits information from more than one data document to be included in a main document. Takes only one form:

«NEXT»

☐ «INCLUDE *document name*»

Causes Word to print an entire second document—*document name*—as an insert to your main document. For example:

«INCLUDE japan.doc»

Preparing the Data Document

Conceptually, it helps to think of a data document as a table in which each row is a record and each column is a category of information called a field. A single row (which is a paragraph of one or more lines on the screen) is a series of fields that provides the main document with the variable information needed to print one merge ("personalized") document.

To create a data document, type a first paragraph that is composed only of field names, separated by commas. For example, a data document for a form letter might have this first paragraph naming seven fields in order:

TITLE,FIRST,LAST,STREET,CITY,STATE,ZIP

Each remaining paragraph in a data document is a record that follows the scheme laid down in the first paragraph. For example, the second paragraph (first record) might be

Mr.,Harold,Bethyname,3 W. Main,Bethlehem,PA,18018

The data document can contain any number of such records, but the fields must always be in the same order. Word uses each record to print a customized version of the main document.

If the information in a field contains a comma, enclose the field in quotation marks. For instance, if Mr. Bethyname is an attorney you want to flatter, his record might be

,Harold,"Bethyname, Esq.",3 W. Main,
Bethlehem,PA,18018

You can leave a field blank, but you can't omit its comma. In the preceding example, note that *Mr.* has been dropped (because it's improper to use *Esq.* with any other title) but that the comma remains.

The File Menu's Print Merge Command

To merge the records of a data document into a main document and print the results, load the main document, choose File Print Merge (Alt+FM), and then choose the Print command button in the resulting dialog box.

If you prefer to save merged documents as a file instead of sending them to the printer, choose the New Document command button in the Print Merge dialog box. This brings up another dialog box, in which you type a name for the resulting document and then press Enter. The command prints on disk a single document that contains as many merge documents as there were records, each starting on a new page.

To print some records but not all, choose the Records option in the Print Merge dialog box and type the numbers of the records you want to print in the text box. Separate numbers with commas, and use hyphens to identify sequences of records. For example, *1,4-7,9* merges records 1, 4 through 7, and 9.

See also: Forms; Printing.

Microsoft Excel

See: Linking spreadsheets.

Microsoft Multiplan

See: Linking spreadsheets.

Microsoft Windows

See: Clipboard; Linking graphics.

Microsoft Works

See: Linking spreadsheets.

Mode

Mode is a DOS command used to configure your computer to work with a printer or with certain displays (monitors). For example, if you use a serial printer (connected to either of the serial ports, COM1: or COM2:) you must use the Mode command to tell your computer how to communicate with it. The following instruction, whether typed at a DOS prompt or included in an AUTOEXEC.BAT file, lets Word communicate with a LaserJet II printer connected to the first serial port:

```
mode com1:96,n,8,1,p
```

In the above instruction, the *96* specifies a baud (communications) rate of 9600, the *n* means "no parity checking," the *8* means "8 databits," the *1* means "1 stop bit," and the *p* tells the computer to continuously retry sending to the printer, even when the printer does not appear (to the computer) to be ready.

The following instruction tells the computer to continuously retry sending a document to a parallel printer connected to the first printer port:

```
mode lpt1:,,p
```

Including this instruction in your AUTOEXEC.BAT file is
a good idea if you print documents that include graphics or
extensive formatting. Printing such documents can require
time-consuming calculations by a printer—so time-
consuming that a parallel port not configured with the
Mode command can lose patience and stop trying to send
information to the printer.

Mouse

The Microsoft Mouse provides an alternative way to give
instructions to your computer. You roll it on your desktop a
few inches in one direction or another to move a special
pointer around the screen. The pointer might be a rectangular or square cursor if you are operating in a text mode, and
it assumes any of several shapes—most often an arrow—if
you are operating in a graphics mode (and in some text
modes).

Before you can use the mouse, you must install it. Each
time you start or reboot your computer, the mouse software
must be run. One particular version of the mouse program,
MOUSE.SYS, is run through your CONFIG.SYS file.
The other version, MOUSE.COM, can be run by typing
mouse at a DOS prompt or by including the word in an
AUTOEXEC.BAT file.

To use the mouse, you press either or both of its buttons.
Sometimes you hold down a button as you move (''drag'')
the mouse pointer, but most often you quickly press and
release (''click'') one or both buttons. For some operations,
you quickly press and release the left button twice in succession (''double-click'').

For some tasks the keyboard is more efficient than the
mouse; for other tasks the mouse is more efficient. Generally, the mouse is superior for jobs that lend themselves to
pointing—for example, selecting (highlighting) a passage
of text.

Choosing Commands

Point at a menu name on the menu bar and click the left
mouse button. On the drop-down menu, point at the desired
choice and click the left button again. To leave the menu
without executing a command, click the left mouse button
when the mouse pointer is in the text area of your screen.

To make choices in a dialog box, point to the desired choice
and click the left mouse button. To see a list of choices in a
drop-down list box, point at the downward-facing arrow
that follows the box and click the left mouse button. To execute the command, click on the OK button; to cancel the
command, click on the Cancel button.

Selecting Text

To select a character, point to it, click the left button, and
drag the mouse to the right until the character is highlighted. To select a word, point to it and click the right button or double-click the left button. To select a sentence,
point to any part of it, hold down the Ctrl key, and click the
left button. To select a line, point to the left of it in the
selection bar and click the left button. To select a paragraph, point to the selection bar and click the right button.
To select the entire document, point to the selection bar and
click both buttons at once.

Scrolling

To scroll through your document with the mouse, use the
vertical and horizontal scroll bars. These can be turned on
or off in the dialog box of the View Preferences command.
Each has a small box—called the *scroll box*—which marks
relative vertical or horizontal position in your document.

To scroll up in your document line by line, point to the
upward-facing arrow at the top of the vertical scroll bar
and either click the left mouse button (to scroll up one line)
or hold down the left mouse button (to scroll continuously).
To scroll down line by line, point to the downward-facing
arrow.

To scroll up or down screen by screen, click the left mouse
button on the vertical scroll bar—click above the scroll box
to scroll up, or below the scroll box to scroll down.

To scroll horizontally in a document that has lines wider than the window, click on the left-facing or right-facing arrow on the horizontal scroll bar (to scroll character by character) or click to the left or right of the scroll box to scroll by one-third of the screen width.

To scroll to an approximate vertical or horizontal position in your document, drag the scroll box to a relative position on the scroll bar. To move to the middle of your document, for example, drag the vertical scroll box to a position halfway down the vertical scroll bar.

Moving Text

To move text to a new location, select it, point to the destination with the mouse, hold down Ctrl, and click the right button. To copy the selection instead of moving it, hold down Ctrl and Shift and click the right button.

Manipulating Windows

To turn the ruler on or off, point to the ribbon/ruler icon at the top of the vertical scroll bar (it looks like an upside-down T) and click the left mouse button. To turn the ribbon on or off, click the right button instead.

To maximize or restore a window, click on the double-headed arrow in the upper-right corner of the window.

To split a window into two panes, double-click on the split icon (=), also located in the upper-right corner. To close the split, double-click on it again. To adjust the position of the split line, point to the split icon and drag it up or down.

To switch to another window that is visible on the screen, click the left mouse button on any portion of it.

To change the size of a window, point to the lower-right corner of the window border and drag it to the desired position.

To move the active window, drag either the window title bar or the left window border.

To close the active window, click on the small rectangle in the upper-left corner of the window.

Setting Tab Stops and Indents

When the ruler is displayed, set a tab stop by pointing with
the mouse to a location in the ruler and clicking the left
button. You can control tab-stop alignment and dictate
whether it will have a leader character by first clicking as
many times as are necessary on the symbols for tab stop
and leader character. These symbols are at the left end of
the ruler. For example, −L indicates a left-aligned tab stop
with a hyphen as leader character. To remove an existing
tab stop, drag the tab stop off the ruler and release. To
move a paragraph's indent, point (in the ruler) to the symbol for the indent, hold down the right mouse button, and
drag the pointer to the desired new position.

See also: AUTOEXEC; CONFIG.SYS; Ribbon; Ruler.

Moving text

To move text from one location to another, select (highlight) it, choose Edit Cut (Alt+ET) to delete it to the scrap,
select the location where you want it to appear, and choose
Edit Paste (Alt+EP).

See also: Copying text to the scrap; Deleting text; Inserting text; Mouse.

Multiplan

See: Linking spreadsheets.

Multiplying numbers

See: Math.

New column

To force Word to begin a new column, hold down the Shift
and Ctrl keys and press Enter, or choose Break from the
Insert menu, choose the Column option button, and press
Enter. This inserts a new-column character, which on the
screen looks just like a new-page character (a series of dots
across the screen).

New line

Hold down Shift and press Enter to start a new line without
starting a new paragraph. Doing so inserts a new-line character, which displays on the screen as a down-facing arrow,
but only if the Paragraph Marks check box of the View
menu's Preferences dialog box is turned on.

See also: Paragraph mark.

New page

See: Page breaks.

NORMAL.GLY

Give the special name NORMAL.GLY to a glossary file containing macros and glossary text entries you use frequently. Word loads this file into the glossary when you start a session, so its entries are always available.

Different document disks (and directories on a fixed disk) can have different NORMAL.GLY files, making it possible to dedicate disks and directories to different purposes, each with its own macros and other glossary entries.

If NORMAL.GLY is in a directory with the Word program and if the directory is in the path, both Word and the NORMAL.GLY glossary file are available for use in any other directory unless that directory has a NORMAL.GLY of its own.

If you are running Word on a network and do not have a NORMAL.GLY in your own Word directory or document directory, the network's version will be loaded whenever you start Word.

If a macro is named AUTOEXEC and is stored in NORMAL.GLY, it runs whenever you start Word.

See also: AUTOEXEC; Glossary; Macros; Path.

NORMAL.STY

NORMAL.STY is the name given a style sheet that can, with appropriate formatting, in effect redefine Word's default formatting. NORMAL.STY formats documents stored in the same directory as NORMAL.STY unless you deliberately detach the style sheet or attach a different one. Because such dedicated styles as Section Normal and Paragraph Normal automatically format elements of a

document, NORMAL.STY is a powerful tool for creating
documents of uniform appearance.

If you place a NORMAL.STY in your Word directory, it
will be available for documents in all directories, provided
there is no NORMAL.STY in the directory containing the
document.

See also: Attaching a style sheet; Automatic styles;
Detaching a style sheet; Styles; Style sheets.

Numbering

Word offers two ways to number paragraphs: a simple way,
and a more sophisticated way that also lets you number
(and cross-reference) other kinds of items, such as figures
or tables.

The Simple Way

To update the numbering of paragraphs that begin with
numbers, select (highlight) the paragraphs and choose
Utilities Renumber (Alt+UR), set the following fields of
the dialog box as appropriate, and press Enter:

Renumber Paragraphs Choose All to update existing
numbering, or Remove to remove all the numbers/letters
that start paragraphs.

Restart Sequence Do you want renumbering to begin at 1
(or I or i or A or a)? If you check this box, Word restarts
the sequences of numbers. If you do not, Word accepts the
first number in the selection and continues the sequence
upward.

Word recognizes and updates a number or letter, provided
it is followed by a period (.) or a close parenthesis ()) that
is in turn followed by a space or tab character and some
text. The Renumber command won't update a number that
isn't followed by punctuation and text. Also, the number or
letter must begin a paragraph, except that it may be preceded by spaces, tab characters, and/or an open parenthesis

(( ). As examples, Word recognizes and updates all of these: 4, 4), (4), IV., IV), (IV), iv., iv), (iv), A., A), (A), a., a), (a), 2.3, 2.3), and (2.3). Word renumbers using the numbering scheme (such as Roman or Arabic) and punctuation that it first encounters.

Note: *If you use Utilities Renumber while in outline view, all paragraphs receive numbers, not just those that had numbers to begin with. In other words, in outline view Word doesn't just renumber, it numbers.*

The Sophisticated Way

To create a numbered series that can appear anywhere within a document, first choose a name for the series. For example, it might be ''figure'' if you want to number a series of figures.

Then, at each place in the document where a number should print, type the name of the series followed by a colon, and press the F3 key. In our example, you would type *figure:* and press F3.

Word replaces the series name with a special character called a *sequence holder,* which appears on screen as the series name enclosed in parentheses. In our example, the sequence holder would appear as *(figure:)* but would print as a number; the first occurrence as number *1*, the second as *2*, and so forth.

To have Word count an item but not print its number, type the series name with two colons instead of one. For instance, if you type *table:* and press F3, then *table::* and press F3 again, and *table:* and press F3 yet again, it will appear on screen as *(table:) (table::) (table:)* and print as *1 3*.

To adjust the number, type two colons followed by one less than the desired number. For example, *table::7* resets the sequence to *7* but does not print, so the next *(table:)* will print as *8*.

A document can contain at least 10 different series names, each with independent numbering.

Word also numbers footnote references, lines, and pages, using other features.

See also: Cross-references; Footnotes; Line numbers; Outlining; Page numbers; Paragraph formatting; Section formatting.

Opening a document

To open a document, choose File Open (Alt+FO or Alt+Ctrl+F2), type the name of the document, and press Enter. You needn't type the extension if the extension is .DOC. (Word assigns this extension to documents when it saves them.)

The Files list box displays a list of available documents. To see filenames other than those ending in .DOC, choose the Style Sheets option (to view documents with the extension .STY) or the All Files option in the Show Files field. To see a list of documents in other directories or drives, use the Directories list box to choose another path.

To read the document without fear of accidentally changing it, turn on the Read Only check box.

Note: *In earlier versions of Word, "opening" a document was referred to as "loading" a document.*

See also: Directories and subdirectories; File management; Path; Wildcards.

Opening windows

See: Windows.

Option buttons

Option buttons (sometimes called *radio buttons*) are dialog
box fields that allow you to choose from a discrete number
of choices. Option buttons are represented by parentheses.
The chosen option is marked by a dot in the parentheses.

To choose a different option, use the direction keys or press
Alt plus the accelerator key of the desired option.

Options

The functions performed by the Options command in
version 5.0 of Word are now performed by a variety of
commands.

See: Layout view; Outlining; Printing (Options, Printer
Setup); Ruler; Utilities Customize; View Preferences.

Organize

See: Outlining.

OS/2

For the most part, Word runs under OS/2 as it does under
DOS. A few points of difference are as follows: Under
OS/2, some of Word's utility programs must be run in the
DOS compatibility box; the CAPTURE program that cap-
tures screen images won't work under OS/2; and mouse

support isn't completely available under OS/2, in either protected mode or the DOS compatibility box.

However, if you install OS/2 on a system that already runs DOS and Word, perform the following steps to ensure that Word runs properly: 1) Add the line *IOPL=Yes* to the CONFIG.SYS file; 2) Replace the OS/2 file POINTDD.SYS by copying the POINTDD.SYS file from the Word disk.

Outlining

To enter or exit outline view, choose View Outline (Alt+VO or Shift+F2). When you are in outline view, a dot appears to the left of the word Outline on the drop-down View menu.

In outline view, you can "collapse" out of view some or all document text, leaving only document headings. The headings are indented to reflect their level (relative importance). The outline view facility lets you examine and manipulate the structure of your document.

Once in outline view, you can work in one of two modes: outline edit or outline organize. To move between them, hold down Shift and press F5.

Working in the Outline Modes

When you enter outline view, you're in outline edit mode. This mode lets you write or edit headings or text that isn't collapsed out of view. You can't select parts of more than one paragraph. (In outline edit, the word Text or Level appears in the screen's lower-left corner, where page numbers are displayed when you're in regular document view.)

The outline organize mode lets you manipulate the structure of the document by manipulating the structure of the outline; when you move an outline heading, lower-level headings and text under it also move. You can't select anything less than full paragraphs. (In outline organize, the word ORGANIZE appears in the screen's lower-left corner.)

In either outline mode, headings that have other headings collapsed under them are marked in the selection bar with +. Headings that have only text collapsed under them are marked with *t*. Text that is "expanded" (not collapsed) is marked with *T*.

The simplest and fastest way to make a paragraph into a heading or to adjust a heading to a different level is to format with styles. A Word style sheet can include up to seven "automatic" paragraph styles that are dedicated to headings. These styles have the names Heading 1 through Heading 7, and by convention their key codes are H1 through H7. In document view, these Heading level styles can apply any combination of paragraph and character formatting to headings. In outline view, Word understands the paragraphs to be headings, and so they are displayed in outline form with appropriate levels of indentation.

Another way to tell Word that a paragraph is a heading is to enter outline view, select the paragraph, and hold down Ctrl and press 9 or 0. The first use of Ctrl+9 turns the paragraph into a heading. Thereafter, Ctrl+9 "promotes" the heading to a higher level, and Ctrl+0 "demotes" the heading to a lower level. (This promotion-demotion method enforces rules of proper outlining by refusing, for example, to place a level 3 heading under a level 1 heading without an intervening level 2 heading.)

A key to understanding outlining is to recognize that the headings in the outline are the same headings that appear in the document itself. When you change a heading in one place, it changes in the other. Consequently, outlining is best suited to structured documents, such as reports or books that use levels of headings.

If you want to use headings to outline and organize a document but you don't want some or all of the headings to print, format them as hidden text. Then, choose View Preferences, and turn on the Hidden Text check box. Then choose File Print Options, and turn off the Hidden Text check box.

For a complete list of keys that perform tasks in outline view, see the Appendix.

Outlining with Style Sheets

To put the outlining feature to work in an easy and useful way, attach a style sheet that includes Paragraph Heading level styles and use those styles to format your document's headings while still in document view. Then, to see your document in outline form, hold down Shift and press F2 to switch to outline view. You might see text as well as headings at this point, in which case you should hold down the Shift and Ctrl keys and press a number from 1 to 7 on your main keyboard (*not* a function key, or a number on the numeric keypad). If you press the number 1, only first-level headings will appear on the screen. If you press 2, only first-level and second-level headings will appear, and so forth. At this point, all headings show, but text paragraphs don't. Select the heading at which you wish to work, and use the keys listed in the Appendix under "Outlining" or hold down Shift and press F2 to return to document view.

Including an Outline in a Document

To include an outline as part of a document, don't use outline view. Instead, use traditional formatting on the individual paragraphs of the outline. Styles are invaluable for this, because once you've defined a paragraph style for each of your levels of outline heading, you need type only a key code to use the formatting again and again.

See also: Appendix; Applying a style; Automatic styles; Numbering; Styles; Style sheets.

Overtyping

To turn the overtype mode on or off, press Alt+F5. (You can also use the Ins key, provided the Use INS for Overtype Key check box of the Utilities menu's Customize dialog box is turned on.) When overtype is on, the letters OT appear on the screen's status line.

Word normally is in insert mode, in which new characters typed in the middle of a line push the existing letters to the right. In overtype mode, however, new characters replace existing characters—that is, overtype them.

Page breaks

To control where Word breaks from one page to another during printing, either type a new-page character by holding down Ctrl and pressing Enter, or use Utilities Repaginate Now (Alt+UP) and turn on the Confirm Page Breaks check box.

By default, Word won't print only one line of a multiline paragraph at the top or the bottom of a page. To override this condition, turn off the Widow/Orphan Control check box of the Utilities menu's Customize dialog box. To tell Word to keep a particular paragraph from breaking across two pages, format it with the Together check box of the Format menu's Paragraph dialog box turned on. To tell Word to keep the end of a paragraph on the same page as the beginning of the next paragraph, format the first paragraph with the With Next check box of the Paragraph dialog box turned on.

When Word places a page break in a document, the page break appears on the screen as a widely spaced dotted line (actually, a row of periods separated from one another by spaces, like this: . . . .). Such a page break can move up or down as you edit the document if you have Background Pagination on (*See:* Utilities Customize) or if you repaginate. When you tell Word where to place a page break, it appears on the screen as a tightly spaced dotted line (a row of periods without spaces between them, like this: ....). Such a page break is fixed unless you move or delete it.

See also: Paragraph formatting (Format Paragraph); Repaginating.

Page formatting

See: Section formatting.

Page layout

See: Section formatting.

Page margins

See: Section formatting (Format Margins).

Page numbers

To include page numbers in a printed document, either use Insert Page Numbers (Alt+IU) or insert the reserved glossary name *page* in a header or footer. To move to a specific page number, use Edit Go To (Alt+EG).

See also: Cross-references; Glossary (Using Reserved Glossary Names); Headers and footers; Jumping through a document; Section formatting.

Pagination

See: Repaginating.

Paragraph formatting

Paragraph formatting establishes such line formatting as indentation, spacing, and alignment. Paragraph formatting affects entire paragraphs and applies to as many paragraphs as are selected (highlighted) when you apply the formatting. On the screen, paragraphs generally look much the way they will print. This accuracy decreases when you format characters to print in more than one size, however, because the screen shows all characters as the same size.

Paragraph formatting is stored in the (usually invisible) paragraph mark that ends each paragraph. Delete the mark and you delete the formatting.

Four commands on the Format menu control paragraph formatting. The Paragraph command governs such elements as indentation, alignment, and line spacing. The Borders command controls whether a paragraph is boxed in whole or in part. The Tabs command governs the placement of tab stops in a paragraph. (*See:* Tabs.) The Position command lets you fix a paragraph to a particular place on a page. (*See:* Absolute positioning.)

If no style sheet is attached to a document, Word uses a "normal" paragraph format unless other formatting is deliberately applied. The "normal" paragraph has flush-left (nonjustified) alignment, no indentations, single-spacing with six lines to the inch, no extra blank lines before or after the paragraph, and no borders or tab stops other than Word's evenly spaced default tab stops. If a style sheet is attached to a document, the normal paragraph formatting is governed by the style sheet's Paragraph Normal style.

To format a paragraph, first select at least one character in it; then apply the formatting either directly, with a built-in format or one of the four paragraph formatting commands, or indirectly, through the use of a paragraph style.

Format Paragraph

Choose the Paragraph command (Alt+TP), set the following dialog box fields as appropriate, and press Enter:

Alignment How do you want the lines of the paragraph to align? The Left setting produces normal typewriter format: The lines are flush left, with a ragged right margin. The Center setting causes each line to be centered within the paragraph's indentations. The Right setting places the lines flush right, with a ragged left margin. The Justified setting causes each line to be flush left and each line except the last to be flush right. Spaces between the letters and/or words in each line are adjusted as necessary.

(Indents) From Left How far from the left page margin do you want the paragraph to be positioned? The normal setting, 0", aligns the left edge of the paragraph with the left margin of the page.

(Indents) First Line How far from the paragraph's left indent do you want the first line to begin? A popular setting is 0.5", which indents the first line by an additional half inch.

(Indents) From Right How far from the right page margin do you want the paragraph to be positioned? The normal setting, 0", means that a full-length text line reaches the right margin of the page.

(Spacing) Before How much extra vertical space, if any, do you want immediately above the paragraph? To place a blank line between paragraphs, set this field to 1.

(Spacing) After How much extra vertical space, if any, do you want immediately below the paragraph?

(Spacing) Line How much space do you want between the lines of a paragraph? The normal setting is 1 li (one line). If you specify 2, the lines are double spaced. One li equals one-sixth of an inch, or 12 pt (12 points). To add a little extra space between lines, change the line spacing setting from 1 li to 13 pt or 14 pt. You can also type *AUTO* in the line spacing field. This causes Word to adjust line spacing on a line-by-line basis, so that the spacing equals the point size of the largest font on a line.

(Keep Paragraph) Together Do you want to ensure that the entire paragraph prints on one page or in one column? If you check this box, Word moves the whole paragraph to the next page or column rather than splitting it.

(Keep Paragraph) With Next Do you want to ensure that the last line of the paragraph prints on the same page or column as the first two lines of the next paragraph?

Side by Side Do you want paragraphs to print beside each other in separate columns when their widths permit it? Word lets you print paragraphs next to each other in two or more columns, provided that each of the paragraphs involved has been formatted with this check box turned on and that the paragraphs don't overlap each other.

Format Borders

Choose the Borders command (Alt+TB), set the following dialog box fields as appropriate, and press Enter:

Border Type Do you want the paragraph to have a box around it or to have lines on one or more of its sides? If you choose Lines, you also need to turn on one or more of the Top, Bottom, Left, and Right check boxes.

Line Style How heavy do you want the line(s) to be? Accept the default (Normal), or choose Bold, Double, or Thick.

Color The default is Black. If your printer (as indicated by your printer file) permits other colors, press Alt+Down to see a list of choices.

(Background Shading) Color If your printer (as indicated by your printer file) permits colors other than Black, press Alt+Down to see a list of color choices. (This option has an effect only if the Percentage field is not set to 0.)

To extend a box around two or more identically formatted paragraphs that have no extra space between them, select all the paragraphs at once, choose the Format Borders command, set the Border Type field to Lines, turn on the Left and Right check boxes, and press Enter. Now select the first paragraph, choose the Format Borders command, turn on the Top check box, and press Enter. Finally, select the

last paragraph and choose the command again, this time
turning on the Bottom check box. Press Enter, and the
multiparagraph box is complete.

See also: Absolute positioning; Built-in formats; Lines;
Paragraph formatting (Format Borders); Paragraph mark;
Side-by-side text; Styles; Style sheets.

Paragraph mark

To create a paragraph mark, press Enter. This action ends
the paragraph and inserts the mark, which never prints and
which is invisible on the screen as long as the View Preferences command's Paragraph Marks check box is turned
off. When the mark is visible on the screen, it looks like
this: ¶. The paragraph mark is a character just as letters,
numbers, and punctuation marks are characters, and as
such it can be selected, copied, or deleted.

A paragraph mark stores the paragraph formatting for all
text back to the previous mark. If a mark is deleted, the formatting of the paragraph is deleted and the text joins the
following paragraph, where it is governed by the formatting
of that paragraph's mark.

See also: ASCII files; New line; Paragraph formatting.

Path

In the context of personal computing and Word, the term
path has two related meanings. The path is the drive letter
and the names of subdirectories leading to a file. It is also
the name of a DOS command that lets you control which
directories DOS should search when looking for a file.

To see your current default path, choose File Open Options.

When you want to open a document or a style sheet that isn't in the current directory, type the path leading to the file as if the path were part of the filename. For example, if the document SAYWHAT is in the JIVE subdirectory of the SLANG subdirectory of the C drive, you can load it from a different directory by choosing File Open, typing *c:\slang\jive\saywhat*, and pressing Enter. To see a listing of documents in the JIVE subdirectory, choose *jive* subdirectory in the Directories list box.

When documents are located in several directories, include in the DOS path the name of the directory containing the Word program. To do this, use the DOS path command, which takes this form: *path=c:\;c:\word;c:\lotus*. When DOS can't find a program in the current directory, it follows the path to try to find it. In this example, the path command tells DOS to look first in the C drive's root directory (*c:*), then in the C drive's WORD subdirectory (*c:\word*), and finally in the C drive's LOTUS subdirectory (*c:\lotus*). Place the path command in the AUTOEXEC.BAT file, so that the path instructions are supplied to DOS each time the computer is started or rebooted.

See also: AUTOEXEC; Directories and subdirectories.

Percentages

See: Math.

Positioning paragraphs

See: Absolute positioning.

PostScript

PostScript is a printer-description language, a sophisticated system which a computer program can use to communicate even elaborate images and layouts to a PostScript-equipped printer or typesetting machine. The best-known PostScript laser printer is the Apple LaserWriter, created for the Apple Macintosh but nicely supported by Word 5.5, too.

A chief advantage of using PostScript is that a wide variety of fonts is available, in virtually any reasonable size. Another advantage is that many typesetting machines, notably those made by Linotronic, can print a finished document directly from a PostScript file. This makes it possible to create a finished document in Word 5.5 and have it typeset directly from your disk—or directly from a computer running Word, when the computer is connected to an appropriate typesetting machine.

To format a document in PostScript fonts, first use File Printer Setup to install the .PRD file POSTSCRP.PRD. (You might first have to run Word's SETUP program to decompress POSTSCRP.PRD and copy it to your Word directory.) Then create your document as usual, using File Print Preview to check on the layout of your work. If you want to use downloadable fonts from Adobe (the vendor of PostScript), install and use the .PRD file PSDOWN.PRD, instead of POSTSCRP.PRD. If Word is connected to a PostScript printer or typesetter, you can print your document directly, using File Print. To print, however, the directory containing the .PRD file must also have a matching .INI file. (For example, POSTSCRP.PRD and POSTSCRP.INI must be together.)

If your printing will be done elsewhere, first use the Print command's To File option to ''print'' the document to disk; then take the resulting print file, along with the .INI file that matches the name of your .PRD file, to the typesetting company.

.PRD file

See: Printer files.

Previewing printing

If your computer display adapter has graphics capability, you can see an on-screen image of pages as they will print with your printer by choosing File Print Preview (Alt+FV). Graphics, columns, headlines, and footnotes will all appear. Be sure that the printer file shown in the Printer File text box of the Printer Setup dialog box matches the printer you'll use to print the document.

After choosing File Print Preview, one or two pages of your document appear on the screen. You can use the PgUp and PgDn keys to scroll through the document and Ctrl+Home and Ctrl+End to jump to the beginning or end of the document.

When you are in print preview mode, not all of the usual menu commands are available, but those which are work the same way as they do in regular document view. In addition, four commands are available only in Print Preview:

File Exit Preview (Alt+FX or Esc) Use this command to exit Preview mode and return to regular document view.

View 1-Page (Alt+V1) Use this command to preview one page of your document at a time.

View 2-Page (Alt+V2) Use this command to preview two pages of your document, side by side.

View Facing Pages (Alt+VF) Use this command to view facing pages side by side.

See also: Jumping through a document; Layout view; Printer files; Printing.

Printer files

The printer file—also called a .PRD file—tells Word
what printer you are using, what its capabilities are, and
how to communicate with it. Install the file for your printer
by running the SETUP program or by choosing File
Printer Setup (Alt+FR) and selecting the appropriate file in
the Files list box. (Word comes with several disks containing printer files, and additional printer files for less common printers are available from Microsoft.)

The printer description tells Word what fonts and sizes are
available for the printer. To see the list of fonts for the installed file, choose Format Character (Alt+TC), and press
Alt plus the Down direction key while you are in the Font
field. The file also contains information Word needs in
order to send graphics to the printer.

If you're adventurous or an experienced programmer, you
can use the MERGEPRD and MAKEPRD programs,
which come with Word, to modify or make .PRD files.
(For an example of using MAKEPRD, *see:* Shading.)

See also: Character formatting; Linking graphics; Paragraph formatting (Format Borders); Printing.

Printing

To print a document, load it into a text window, choose File
Print (Alt+FP), set the following fields of the dialog box as
appropriate, and press Enter:

Print Use this field to choose what you want to print. The
options on the drop-down list are: Document, Summary
Info, Glossary, Style Sheet, and Direct Text. The direct text
option allows you to print text as you type it, using your
computer as a typewriter. When you choose this option and

press Enter, a dialog box appears into which you can type the text to be printed. Press Enter at the end of each line (or choose the Print Text command button), and press Esc (or choose Cancel) when you are finished.

Copies How many copies do you want to print?

Paper Feed Press Alt+Down to see a list of the ways paper can be fed to your printer. Choose Manual if you feed paper to your printer by hand one sheet at a time; this setting prompts Word to pause before every page while you load paper. Choose Continuous if you use fanfold paper or if you have a laser printer with one paper bin. If your printer has more than one bin, choose Bin1, Bin2, or Bin3 to tell Word which bin to use. Bin3 usually is used with an envelope feeder. Choose Mixed to use Bin1 for the first page of a multipage document and Bin2 for subsequent pages (as when you have letterhead stationery in the first bin and nonletterhead paper in the second bin).

To: Printer/File Choose the File option and type a file-name in its associated text box to "print" a document to a file rather than to a printer (for later printing or other use). Use a filename extension other than .DOC to avoid over-writing the original version of your document.

Page Range Choose All to print the entire document and Selection to print only the selected text. To print only certain pages, pick Pages and fill in the Pages text box.

Pages If you chose Pages in the Page Range box, you use this text box to list the page numbers you want printed. Use a comma to separate individual page numbers (1,7); use a hyphen to indicate a range of consecutive pages (2–4). You also can combine the two methods (1–4,7). For a document that has more than one section, place an *s* and the section number after the page number. For example, if you type *1s1-4s2,7s2* in this field, Word prints from page 1 of section 1 to page 4 of section 2, and also prints page 7 of section 2.

Printer Setup

The Printer Setup command can be reached directly from the File menu (Alt+FR) or by choosing the Printer Setup command button in the Print dialog box. The choices in

this command's dialog box indicate your printer and printing needs. Once you set them, you may find little reason
ever to make changes, because Word remembers most settings between editing sessions.

Printer File Which printer description (.PRD) file do you
want Word to use? Type the name of the .PRD file or
choose one from the Files list box. (*See:* Printer files.)

Printer Name If the .PRD file can be used with more than
one model of printer, choose a specific model from this list.

Connect to Which port is your printer connected to? Press
Alt+Down to see a list of choices. For a parallel printer, the
possibilities are LPT1:, LPT2:, LPT3:, and LPT4:. For a
serial printer, the possibilities are COM1:, COM2:, COM3:,
and COM4:, although you might not have all of these available on your system. (With these serial choices, you must
also use the Mode command to tell DOS about your
printer.) If you are using OS/2, you can also type in the
name of any logical network connection.

Paper Feed This field has the same choices as the Paper
Feed field of the Print dialog box (above).

Graphics Resolution What level of graphics resolution
should your printer use? Press Alt+Down to see a list of
resolutions. Choices vary depending on the model: LaserJet
II printers allow 75, 150, and 300 dpi (dots per inch).
Higher numbers give better resolution but require more
printer memory and more time to print. Graphics resolution can also be set in the Print Options dialog box.

Use Print Queue Do you want the document to be sent to a
"queue" file so that you can continue using Word while it
prints? (*See:* Queued printing.)

Skip Downloading Fonts Do you want to speed up your
print job by preventing Word from downloading fonts to
your printer?

Options

The Print Options dialog box, which is reached by choosing the Options command button in the Print dialog box, allows you to provide Word with further specifications on how you want your document to be printed.

Draft To print at high speed, in the default font and without microspace justification, turn on this check box.

Duplex Turn on this check box if your printer can print on both sides of a page without your intervention and you want to use this capability.

Summary Info Before printing a document, do you want Word to print the document's summary information on a separate piece of paper? (*See:* Document retrieval.)

Hidden Text Do you want characters that are formatted as "hidden" to print? If you check this box, hidden characters also will appear on screen when you are in layout view. (*See:* Hidden text; Layout view.)

Graphics Resolution Graphics resolution can also be set in the Printer Setup dialog box.

See also: ASCII files; Merging; Mode; Paragraph formatting (Format Borders); Previewing printing; Queued printing; Repaginating.

Print merge

See: Merging.

Print preview

See: Previewing printing.

Product support

Microsoft offers free (but not toll-free) telephone support
for Microsoft Word owners. The number is (206) 454-2030.
Hours are 6 A.M. to 6 P.M. Pacific time (9 A.M. to 9 P.M.
Eastern time).

Proposed response

When a command field is displayed, Word often proposes
a response, which reflects the current condition of a document or of Word's configuration. For instance, Word generally proposes a top margin of 1 inch in the Top field of the
Section Margins dialog box. You can accept a proposed response or change it.

See also: Dialog box.

Queued printing

To print a document while continuing to use Word, choose
File Printer Setup (Alt+FR) and turn on the Use Print
Queue check box. Then use File Print. Word pauses while
it writes a print-file version of the document to a temporary
"queue" file on the Word disk or directory. Once printing
begins, you can use Word, although performance will be
degraded—perhaps substantially.

To control the printing of queued documents, choose File
Print Queue (Alt+FQ) and then choose one of the following
four options:

Pause Temporarily suspends queued printing.

Continue Resumes queued printing that has been suspended.

Restart File Begins printing the document again, repeating pages that have already printed.

Stop Queue Cancels queued printing, erasing the temporary disk file in which the queue is stored.

To use queued printing, ample free space must be available on the Word disk or directory.

See also: Printing.

Quitting Word

See: Exiting Word.

Recording a macro

See: Macros.

Recording a style

To record an example of formatting in a document, storing it as a style in a style sheet, choose Format Record Style (Alt+TR), set the following fields of the dialog box as appropriate, and press Enter:

Key Code Type a key code of one or, preferably, two characters. This is the code you'll use later—by typing it after pressing Ctrl+Y—to apply the style to text.

Style Type Do you want this to be a character, paragraph, or section style?

Remark If you want, type an explanatory comment of up to 28 characters.

Style I.D. For each kind of style (character, paragraph, and section), there is a set number of possible styles, each of which is called a "style I.D." Automatic styles—those reserved for specific tasks—use a name as the I.D.; non-automatic styles generally use a number. For example, the automatic style Paragraph Normal has the type Paragraph and the style I.D. Paragraph Normal, and the style Character 1 has the type Character and the style I.D. 1. Press Alt+Down to see a list of I.D. names. Any I.D. that already is used by a style in the current style sheet, and hence is unavailable, is followed by parentheses containing the style's key code.

See also: Applying a style; Automatic styles; Styles; Style sheet window.

Redlining

See: Revision marks.

Remark

See: Recording a style; Styles; Style sheet window (Edit Menu Commands).

Renaming a document

See: File Management (Rename).

Repaginating

Word repaginates automatically if you want it to. In other words, it constantly updates a document's page breaks and page numbering as you write and edit. This occurs as long as the Background Pagination check box of Utilities Customize is turned on. To repaginate when this check box is not turned on, choose Utilities Repaginate Now (Alt+UP). To preview page breaks and possibly adjust them, turn on the Confirm Page Breaks check box before pressing Enter.

If you ask to confirm Word's choices, it pauses at each potential page-break location and displays the following message: *Press Enter to confirm page break or use direction keys to reposition it.* Press Enter to accept the proposed location, or use the Up direction key to choose a point higher on the page and then press Enter. Word inserts a new-page character at that point.

Word also repaginates a document when you print it or run certain other commands, such as Insert Index, Insert Table of Contents, or Print Preview.

See also: Page breaks; Printing; Utilities Customize.

Repeating an edit or macro

To repeat the last edit or macro, press F4 or choose Repeat from the Edit menu. For example, if you format one character as hidden text, you can format a second character as hidden by selecting the character and pressing F4.

To repeat the last search, whether for text or formatting, hold down the Shift key and press F4.

See also: Searching for formats and styles; Searching for text; Undoing an edit.

Replacing formats and styles

To search a portion of a document and replace one kind of formatting with another, first select (highlight) the portion of the document in which you want the replacements to occur. Be sure no characters are selected if you want the entire document examined. Then choose Edit Replace (Alt+EE), and turn on the Confirm Changes check box if you want Word to check with you before each replacement is made. Next, choose Replace Formatting Only, and then choose one of three options: Character, Paragraph, or Style.

Character

Choose Character to search for a combination of character formats that you want replaced with another combination. The dialog box you are presented with contains the same choices as the Format menu's Character dialog box, plus one more: Replace With. Choose the combination of character formats that you want to replace, then choose Replace With. Word displays another dialog box, in which you choose the combination of formats you want. When done, press Enter.

Paragraph

Choose Paragraph to search for a combination of paragraph formats that you want to replace with another combination. The choices in the resulting dialog box are the same as those of the Format menu's Paragraph dialog box, plus one more: the Replace With command button. Choose the combination of paragraph formats that you want to replace, and choose Replace With. Word displays another dialog box, in which you choose the combination of formats you want. When ready, press Enter.

Style

Choose Style to search for instances of text formatted with
a specific style that you want to format with a different
style. The Style option works with character, paragraph,
and section styles, but you can replace a style only with a
style of the same type. In the Keycode to Search for text
box, type the key code of the style you want to replace. In
the Replace with text box, type the key code of the replacement style. Then press Enter.

See also: Character formatting (Format Character); Paragraph formatting (Format Paragraph); Searching for formats and styles.

Replacing text

To search a document for specific text and replace occur-
rences of it with other specific text, first be sure no characters are selected (highlighted) and then choose Edit Replace
(Alt+EE). (To search only a portion of the document, highlight that portion.) Set the following fields as appropriate
and press Enter:

Text to Search for Type the text you want to find and
replace. Word accepts up to 256 characters, including numbers and punctuation marks. If you've used either Edit
Replace or Edit Search during the same editing session,
Word proposes the previous text entry.

To search for special characters, you must precede them
with a caret (^ or Shift+6). For example, to search for a
question mark (?), which is a "wildcard" that represents
any character, you must precede it with a caret in the text
field: ^?.

Other special characters are as follows:

■ ^- (hyphen) represents optional (nonrequired) hyphens
  you've inserted (by using Utilities Hyphenate or by holding down Shift and Ctrl and pressing the hyphen key).

- ^c represents new-column characters.

- ^d represents either section marks or new-page marks, both of which are formatting characters.

- ^n represents new-line characters.

- ^p represents paragraph marks.

- ^s represents nonbreaking spaces, which you insert between words (by holding down Shift and Ctrl and pressing the Spacebar) to ensure that a new line won't begin between the words.

- ^t represents tab characters, which you create by pressing the Tab key.

- ^w represents any and all spaces and spacing characters in your document, including Spacebar spaces, tab characters, paragraph marks, new-line characters, section marks, new-page marks, and nonbreaking spaces.

Replace with Type the text that you want to have replace the material in the Text to Search for text box. Again, you can specify up to 256 characters, and you can use the previously noted special characters, with the exception of ^w.

Whole Word Do you want Word to search for whole words only? If you check this box, Word stops only at matching text it interprets as a whole word (that is, a collection of characters with either spaces or punctuation marks at both ends). If you do not check this box, Word replaces the characters you specify, even if they are fragments of other words.

Match Upper/Lowercase Do you want Word to seek only text whose use of uppercase and lowercase exactly matches the characters you've typed in the Text to Search for field?

Confirm Changes Do you want Word to ask your permission before making each replacement? If you check this box, Word stops each time it finds the designated text, highlights it, and displays the message *Do you want to replace the selection?*

See also: Searching for text; Wildcards.

Return key

See: Enter key.

Revision marks

To cause Word to keep track of your additions and dele-
tions to a document, use Utilities Revision Marks
(Alt+UM).

The revision-marks feature, also called "redlining," by
default marks added text with an underline and deleted text
with a strikethrough. This practice conforms to typical law-
office and legislative requirements. If you're running Word
in text mode on a color system, you can use View Preferences to adjust the colors used to represent underlines and
strikethroughs. On a monochrome (noncolor) system that
doesn't have graphics, both underlines and strikethroughs
show as underlines. If you are in show layout mode, revision marks will appear on screen only for the first column;
but they will print for all columns.

The following choices are available in the Mark Revisions
dialog box:

Mark Revisions Turn the revision-marks feature on and
off with this check box.

Mark New Text With How do you want new characters
distinguished from existing characters? Underline is the
default. However, if you are using a nongraphics, noncolor
screen, you might want to set this field to Bold or Uppercase, because otherwise your screen will mark both dele-
tions and insertions with an underline. You can also choose
Double Underline or Nothing.

Revision Bars Do you want to use revision bars? If so, in
which margin do you want them to appear? Revision bars

are vertical bars placed next to lines which have been changed, making revisions easier to spot.

Search Use this command button to search for the next instance of revised text. To selectively accept proposed revisions, you can use the Search command button to highlight an instance of revised text. Then choose either Accept Revisions or Undo Revisions.

Accept Revisions Choose this command button if, after reviewing a marked copy of your document, you want to accept the revisions, thereby making the proposed changes permanent. The command deletes struckthrough text, removes underlining (or other special formatting) from the newly inserted text, and removes revision bars from the margins. To accept revisions for only a portion of the document, select (highlight) the desired portion before choosing the command.

Undo Revisions Choose this command button if, after reviewing a marked copy of your document, you want to abandon the proposed changes. The command removes the strikethrough from text marked for deletion, deletes newly inserted text, and removes revision bars from the margins. It is the opposite of Accept Revisions. If you wish to abandon changes for only a portion of the document, select (highlight) the desired portion before choosing the command.

See also: Colors on the screen; Deleting text; Layout view.

Ribbon

The ribbon lets you monitor and easily control important aspects of the formatting of your document. Only one ribbon exists, no matter how many document windows are open. You toggle the ribbon on or off by using the Ribbon command (holding the Alt key and pressing VB) or by positioning the mouse cursor over the ⊥ symbol in the right border of the screen and clicking the right mouse button.

The ribbon reflects the formatting of the selection in the active window. Typically, the ribbon looks like this:

```
 Style:[Normal (NP).......]↓  Font:[modern a......]↓  Pts:[12.]↓  Bld Ital Ul
```

There are six elements in the ribbon: the Style, Font, and Pts drop-down list boxes, and the Bld, Ital, and Ul character-formatting indicators.

Style of the paragraph The Style drop-down list box reflects and lets you change the style of the selected paragraph.

To activate the Styles entry field, press Ctrl+S. After the entry field is active, hold down the Alt key and press the Down direction key to see a list of the available styles in the style sheet attached to the active document. The list indicates the I.D. and key code of each of the available styles. To apply a style to the selected text, double-click on the style's name with the mouse, or press the Down direction key until its name is highlighted. Then press Enter. The selected text immediately reflects the style.

If you press Ctrl+S a second time, you reach the Apply Style dialog box—just as if you had used Format Apply Style.

Font of the character The Font drop-down list box lets you monitor or change the font (typeface) of whatever character is selected or is at the location of the cursor. As long as the ribbon is displayed, you can keep track of the font. And even if the ribbon is not displayed, pressing Ctrl+F activates the ribbon temporarily so that you can change the font of the selected text. After the Font entry field is active, press the Down direction key or Alt+Down to choose from among available options.

If you press Ctrl+F a second time, you reach the Character dialog box just as if you had used the Format menu's Character command.

Size of the font To use the ribbon to choose a point size for the font that is formatting the selected text, activate the Pts entry field by holding the Ctrl key and pressing the P key. Once the Pts entry field is active, hold down the Alt key and press the Down direction key to display a drop-down list box of all available font sizes. You can use the Up and Down direction keys to choose a size, such as 14.

To put your choice into effect, double-click on it with the mouse or press the Enter key when it is highlighted.

As with the Fonts list box, you can move directly to the Character dialog box from the Pts entry field: Simply press Ctrl+P when the Pts entry field is active. (This shortcut works only before the drop-down list is displayed.)

Character attributes (Bld Ital Ul) At the far right side of the ribbon are the letters "Bld Ital Ul." Actually three separate abbreviations, these letters stand for "Bold Italic Underlined" and indicate whether one or more of these character-formatting properties are turned on. If the cursor is formatted to be italic—or if instead of having a cursor you have text selected and all of it is formatted to be italic—the letters "Ital" in the ribbon will be emphasized. If the cursor is formatted to be bold or underlined, or if all selected text is bold or underlined, the letters "Bld" and "Ul" will be emphasized, respectively.

If an indicator contains question marks, it means the selected text is inconsistently formatted. For example, if only some of the selected text is bold, the letters "Bld" will display as "B??". Or if all of the selected text is bold but only some of it is italic, the ribbon will display "Bld" in emphasized type and "I???" in nonemphasized type.

See also: Character formatting; Ruler; Style sheets.

Right-alignment

See: Paragraph formatting; Tabs.

Ruler

To turn the ruler at the top of a text window on or off, choose View Ruler (Alt+VR). You can also position the mouse pointer on the ribbon/ruler icon (it looks like an upside-down "T") in the upper-right corner of the window border and click the left button.

Special symbols in the ruler provide information about the formatting of the paragraph that contains the cursor:

[Left indent
]   Right indent
¦   First-line indent
L   Left-aligned tab stop
C   Center-aligned tab stop
R   Right-aligned tab stop
D   Decimal-aligned tab stop
| Vertical line

A period (.), hyphen (-), or underline (_) immediately preceding a tab-stop letter indicates that the tab stop is formatted with that punctuation mark as its leader character. You can set tab stops on the ruler with the mouse or keyboard.

See also: Mouse; Ribbon; Tabs; Window borders.

Running a DOS command or other program

See: DOS commands.

Running heads

See: Headers and footers.

Saving a document

To save a document, choose File Save (Alt+FS or
Alt+Shift+F2). If the document has been saved before,
it is resaved immediately.

If the document hasn't been saved before, you will be taken
to the Save As dialog box to assign a name and file format
to the document. (Alternatively, you can go directly to this
dialog box by pressing Alt+FA or Alt+F2.) Type a name of
up to eight letters in the File Name text box. Word supplies
the filename extension .DOC, so you needn't type an extension. (Thus, type *HAWAII*, not *HAWAII.DOC*.) Leave the
Format list box set to Word, unless you want to create an
ASCII file or write a computer program, in which case set
Format to either Text Only or Text Only w/Breaks, depending on whether or not you want a paragraph mark at the
end of every line. If you're going to transfer your document
to a program that reads Rich Text Format, save with the
Format field set to RTF.

If the Prompt for Summary Info check box of the Utilities
menu's Customize dialog box is turned on, Word presents
a summary sheet to be filled in the first time you save a
document in Word format. If you find that you don't use
summary information, simply turn this check box off.

See also: ASCII files; Autosave; Directories and subdirectories; Path; Saving all files; Summary information.

Saving a glossary file

See: Glossary; Macros.

Saving all files

To save all documents, style sheets, and the current contents of the glossary, choose the Save All (Alt+FE) command. This is a fast way to be sure your work is safely stored on your disk and to free memory when the SAVE indicator appears on the status line.

See also: Saving a document.

Scrap

The scrap is a temporary storage place for text. Transfer selected (highlighted) text to the scrap with Edit Copy (or with the Ctrl+Ins key combination) or Edit Cut (or with the Shift+Del key combination or the Del key, depending on the setting for the Use INS for Overtype key in the Utilities menu's Customize dialog box); transfer text from the scrap to a document with Edit Paste (or with the Shift+Ins key combination). The scrap holds only the text that you most recently copied or deleted.

Text in the scrap is represented inside the scrap brackets, { }, at the bottom of the screen. For instance, if you copy *The cow jumped over the moon*, the scrap brackets show this:

{The...oon}

See also: Copying text to the scrap; Deleting text; Glossary; Inserting text.

Screen borders

See: Window borders.

Scrolling

To move up one line, press the Up direction key. To move
down a line, press the Down direction key. To keep the cursor in its present screen position while scrolling the text
behind it, press the Scroll Lock key before pressing the Up
or Down direction key. Turn off Scroll Lock when you're
through. To scroll through a document one screen at a time,
press the PgUp key (to move toward the beginning of the
document) or the PgDn key (to move toward the end of the
document). To move to the top of the current screen, hold
down Ctrl and press PgUp. To move to the bottom of the
screen, hold down Ctrl and press PgDn. To move to the beginning of the document, hold down Ctrl and press Home.
To move to the end of the document, hold down Ctrl and
press End. For a list of other ways to scroll, see the
Appendix.

See also: Mouse.

Searching for formats and styles

To search a document for the next occurrence of a certain
kind of formatting, first choose Edit Search (Alt+ES) and
make a choice in the Direction box: Up if you want to
search toward the beginning of the document or Down if
you want to search toward the end of the document. Then
choose the Search for Formatting Only command button.

(To search only a portion of the document, first highlight that portion.) When the Search for Formatting dialog box appears, choose one of three options: Character, Paragraph, or Style.

Character

Choose Character to search for a combination of character formats. You will be taken to a dialog box which looks exactly like the Format menu's Character dialog box. Choose the combination of character formats you want and press Enter. To repeat the search, hold down Shift and press F4.

Paragraph

Choose Paragraph to search for a combination of paragraph formats. You will be taken to a dialog box which looks exactly like the Format menu's Paragraph dialog box. Choose the combination of paragraph formats you want and press Enter. To repeat the search, hold down Shift and press F4.

Style

Choose Style to search for text formatted with a specific character, paragraph, or section style. In the command's Keycode to Search for text box, type the key code of the style you seek. Press Enter. To repeat the search, hold down Shift and press F4.

See also: Replacing formats and styles.

Searching for text

To search a document for the next occurrence of specific text, first move the cursor to the location where you want to begin the search and then choose Edit Search (Alt+ES). (To search only a portion of the document, first highlight that portion.) Set the following fields as appropriate and press Enter:

Text to Search for Type the text you seek. Word accepts up to 256 characters, including numbers and punctuation marks. If you've used either Edit Replace or Edit Search during the same editing session, Word proposes the previous text entry. As with Edit Replace, you can search for special characters by preceding them with a caret (^ or Shift+6). (For a list of special characters, *see:* Replacing text.)

Whole Word Do you want Word to search for whole words only? If you check this box, Word stops only at matching text it interprets as a whole word (that is, a collection of characters with either spaces or punctuation marks at both ends). If you do not check this box, Word highlights the characters you specify, even if they are fragments of other words.

Match Upper/Lowercase Do you want Word to seek only text whose use of uppercase and lowercase exactly matches the characters you've typed in the Text to Search for text box?

Direction Do you want Word to search from the selection toward the beginning of the document (Up) or toward the end (Down)?

To repeat a search, hold down Shift and press F4.

To identify documents that contain specific text, choose the Search button from the File Management command on the File menu. Then, to find the text within each document, load the document and use Edit Search.

See also: File management (Search).

Section formatting

Section formatting establishes the design of pages or columns and controls (such as margins, the number of columns on the page, and the printing of page or line numbers).

Documents have only a single section unless you insert section marks to create boundaries between two or more

sections. A section mark is a series of colons extending
across the screen (::::::::::). To insert a section mark,
choose Insert Break (Alt+IB), choose Section in the first
field, and then press Enter.

If no style sheet is attached to a document, Word uses a
built-in section format unless you apply other section formatting. In the U.S. versions of Word the built-in section
format calls for page length of 11 inches and page width of
8.5 inches; no page numbers or line numbers; top and bottom margins of 1 inch each; and left and right margins of
1.25 inches each. If a style sheet is attached to a document,
the default section formatting is that specified in the Section Normal section style, if such a style exists.

To format a section, position the cursor in the section and
then apply the formatting either directly, with Format Section and Format Margins, or indirectly, through the use of a
section style. Insert Page Numbers also affects section formatting, as does Format Header/Footer.

Format Section

This command lets you print two or more columns on a
page, add line numbering to your document, assign rules on
where to begin a new section, and place footnote text either
on the same page as its reference mark or at the end of the
section.

Choose Format Section (Alt+TS), set the following fields
of the dialog box as appropriate, and press Enter:

Number How many columns do you want? (See the Section Start field.)

Spacing If you're using multiple columns, how much space
do you want between each?

Place Footnotes Do you want footnotes printed at the bottom of the appropriate pages or collected at the end of the
section (such as the end of a chapter or an entire
document)?

Add Line Numbers Do you want line numbers printed in
the left margin of the page?

From Text If you turned on the Add Line Numbers field, how far from the text do you want the numbers? (This value must be less than that of the left margin of the document, as specified by Format Margins.)

Count by Do you want numbering to increase by one each time (1, 2, 3, and so on) or by some other increment?

Restart at Do you want numbering to begin on each page, at the start of each section, or to be continuous throughout the document?

Section Start This field controls how Word handles the break between two sections. The default is New Page, which means that Word starts a new page when it reaches the section mark. Choosing Column begins a new column rather than a new page. Choosing Even Page begins a new page on an even-numbered page (leaving a blank odd-numbered page if necessary). Choosing Odd Page begins a new page on an odd-numbered page (leaving a blank even-numbered page if necessary). The tricky (and interesting) choice is Continuous, which causes a section to begin printing on the same page as the previous section, allowing a page to change in its middle from one set of left and right margins to another, or to change numbers of columns, or to switch between having line numbers and not having them. However, the bottom margin of a page does not change, even when a new section starts on it and the new section is set to be Continuous. Furthermore, when a section contains footnotes (including annotations), choosing Continuous has no effect; Word always starts a new page.

Format Margins

Page margins determine the amount of white space around your text, bordering everything except headers and footers, which are printed in the margins. (Paragraph indentations can provide additional bordering, on a paragraph-by-paragraph basis.)

Choose Format Margins (Alt+TM), set the following fields as appropriate, and press Enter:

Width What is the width of the paper?

Height What is the length of the paper?

Top How deep do you want the top page margin?

Bottom How deep do you want the bottom page margin?

If you enter a negative number for Top or Bottom, the margin will not be negative, but rather will be unmovable: It won't adjust itself to make room for a deep header or footer. If no negative sign appears, a margin adjusts itself to accommodate oversized headers and footers.

Gutter Do you want a gutter margin? If so, how much of one? A gutter margin is extra space on the left side of odd-numbered pages and on the right side of even-numbered pages, which allows extra room for binding two-sided printing.

Left How wide do you want the left page margin?

Right How wide do you want the right page margin?

Mirror Margins If you check this box, Word uses the left and right margins specified elsewhere in the dialog box when printing odd-numbered pages, but it reverses them for even-numbered pages.

Use as Default Check this box if you want Word to use the settings of the command as the future default section formatting.

Insert Page Numbers

This command positions and places page numbers on printed pages. Page numbers don't appear on the screen. (As a more flexible alternative, you can print page numbers in a running head by using the reserved glossary name *page*.)

Choose Insert Page Numbers (Alt+IP), set the following fields of the dialog box as appropriate, and press Enter:

Page Number Position Do you want printed page numbers? (Even if you choose None, page numbers are printed if the reserved glossary name *page* is used in a running head.) If so, do you want them printed at the top or bottom of the page, and how far from the top or bottom of the page?

Format Which numbering system do you want to use? The
choices are Arabic numerals (1, 2, 3); uppercase Roman
numerals (I, II, III); lowercase Roman numerals (i, ii, iii);
uppercase letters (A, B, C); and lowercase letters (a, b, c).
(This field, as well as the following one, also governs numbering printed with the special glossary entry *page*.)

Start at Choose Auto to have Word number pages sequen-
tially starting at 1. Otherwise, enter the number at which
you wish page numbering for the current section to begin.

Align Page Number at Do you want to align the page
number at the Left Margin, the Center of the page, or the
Right Margin? You can choose one of these preset options,
or choose From Left Edge and type a specific measurement
in the text box.

Section Styles

If a style sheet containing section styles is attached to your
document, press Ctrl+Y and type the one-character or two-
character key code of the style, such as NS (for Normal
Section).

See also: Footnotes; Headers and footers; Paragraph formatting; Proposed response; Section mark; Styles; Style
sheets.

Section mark

A section mark is a series of colons extending across the
screen (:::::::::::). To insert a section mark in a document,
choose Insert Break (Alt+IB), choose Section in the first
field, and press Enter.

Word places a section mark at the end of a document,
before the end mark, when you use section formatting.
This mark stores the section formatting for the text that
precedes it.

Word also creates a separate section for a table of contents
or index created with Insert Table of Contents or Insert Index. This section, with its own section mark and formatting, follows the section mark that would otherwise end the
document.

See also: Section formatting.

Select

See: Selecting text.

Selecting a column

To select a column, place the cursor at one of the four corners of the column. Then hold down the Shift and Ctrl keys
and press F8 to turn on the column select mode, and press
direction keys until a rectangular area containing the column is highlighted.

Once a column is selected, you can add numbers contained
within it, or you can copy or delete the column to the scrap
for insertion elsewhere in the document (or in a different
document).

See also: Math.

Selecting text

You select, or highlight, text in order to perform an editing
action on it.

To select text, hold down the Shift key and press a direction key (Up, Down, Left, or Right), or press F8 to turn on the extend-selection mode. In this mode, keys that otherwise would move the cursor—such as the direction keys—extend it instead. See the Appendix for a list of keys that extend the cursor.

See also: Mouse; Selecting a column; Selection bar.

Selection

See: Cursor.

Selection bar

The selection bar is a two-character-wide column to the immediate left of text on the screen.

Use it to select text with the mouse. Point to the selection bar with the mouse pointer; click the left button to select a line, the right button to select a paragraph, and both buttons to select an entire document.

Generally, the selection bar is blank, although it displays a caret (^) when the paragraph to the right of it is formatted as a header or footer. Also, in outline view, the selection bar displays T when the paragraph to the right of it is text, t when the paragraph is a heading that has text paragraphs collapsed from view under it, and + when the paragraph is a heading that has other headings collapsed under it.

When in the selection bar, the mouse pointer points to the right.

See also: Copying formatting; Mouse; Outlining; Selecting text; Style bar.

Setting tabs

See: Tabs.

SETUP

To set up Word before you use it for the first time, place the Word Setup disk in your A drive and type *setup*. Then follow the on-screen instructions as the SETUP program readies Word for your use. Before using SETUP, you need to know some basic information about your printer, such as its name and to what computer port it is connected, as well as what kind of display adapter (such as EGA, VGA, or Hercules) is installed in your computer.

Note: *Unlike earlier versions of Word, the files in version 5.5 are compressed. You must run the SETUP command in order to convert these files into a usable form. You cannot just copy your Word files from the factory diskettes to a hard disk and expect the program to run.*

Shading

See: Paragraph formatting (Format Borders).

Show layout mode

See: Layout view.

Side-by-side text

To format paragraphs to print next to each other, choose the
Paragraph command from the Format menu, set the From
Left and From Right text boxes in the dialog box so that the
paragraphs don't overlap, and turn on the Side by Side
check box. For example, if a page 8.5 inches wide has left
and right margins of 1.25 inches each, it leaves 6 inches of
printable width. For the first paragraph, type *0* in the From
Left text box and *3.5* in the From Right field, then turn on
the Side by Side check box. For the second paragraph, set
From Left to *3.5* and From Right to *0*, and turn on the Side
by Side check box. The paragraphs will print beside each
other, separated by a 1-inch gutter. They will not appear
side by side on the screen, however, unless you are using
layout view or print preview.

You also can format paragraphs to print side by side by
using a style sheet that contains paragraph styles for right-
side and left-side printing.

See also: Columns, multiple; Layout view; Paragraph formatting; Previewing printing; Styles.

Sorting

To put paragraphs or lines in alphabetic or numeric order,
first select (highlight) the text to be sorted. Next, choose
Utilities Sort (Alt+UO), set the following dialog box options as appropriate, and press Enter:

Sort Order Word sorts in either Ascending order (*1, 2, 3* or
a, b, c) or Descending order (*9, 8, 7* or *z, y, x*).

Key Type If you choose Alphanumeric, Word sorts the
paragraphs or lines in the following order: special characters (such as % and @) first, then numbers, and then letters.

If you choose Numeric, Word pays attention only to numerals, so that numbered paragraphs, for example, are sorted into sequence but unnumbered paragraphs are not.

Sort Column Only Check this box to sort by columns, or leave it empty to sort by paragraphs. This option is available only if the text was selected using column selection mode (Ctrl+Shift+F8). If entire lines are selected, each line is treated as a paragraph during sorting. If only one column is selected, only the contents of that column are affected by the sort.

Case Sensitive Check this box to place all paragraphs or lines that begin with uppercase letters before paragraphs or lines that begin with lowercase letters. For an ascending sort, the precedence is AaBbCc; for a descending sort, the precedence is cCbBaA. Leave this box empty to ignore case when alphabetizing.

See also: Selecting a column.

Speed formatting keys

See: Built-in formats; Key codes.

Spell-checking

To check the spelling of a word or a portion of the document, select the word or portion and choose Utilities Spelling (Alt+US or F7). Word loads the dictionary specified in the Speller Name field of the Utilities menu's Customize dialog box and immediately begins checking. If everything selected is recognized as being in Word's dictionary, the message *No incorrect words found* appears.

To check spelling for an entire document, place the cursor under a single character and then choose Utilities Spelling. Checking begins from the location of the cursor. If the cursor is not at the beginning of the document, Word pauses when it gets to the end of the document and prompts *Do you want to continue checking spelling from the beginning?* If every word in the document matches an entry in Word's dictionary, the message *No incorrect words found* appears.

When a word is not recognized, the spell-checker displays a dialog box at the bottom of the screen. The unrecognized word is given at the top, and eight command buttons appear at the bottom. The following is a brief description of each command button:

Change

Correct a misspelling with this command. It will replace the unrecognized word with whatever appears in the dialog box's Replace with text box. This can be a correction proposed by the spell-checker, a word you have chosen from the Suggestions list box, or a word you have typed in.

Suggest

Choose this button to have Word display a list of proposed replacements for the unrecognized term. If the Always Suggest check box of the Spelling Options dialog box is turned on, Word automatically displays such a list in the Suggestions list box.

Ignore

Choose Ignore when Word doesn't recognize a word and you want the word left alone (neither corrected nor added to a dictionary).

Add

Choose this command to add the unrecognized word to any of the three kinds of dictionaries that Word can keep. Specify the dictionary in the dialog box's Add to Dictionary drop-down list box before you choose this command. The three kinds of dictionaries are Standard, User, and Document.

Standard Choose Standard to place the word in an update list to the main dictionary used all the time. A disadvantage: The more words you have in the Standard dictionary, the longer Word takes to check the spelling of any document. (Microsoft dictionaries are available in French, Spanish, German, Dutch, Swedish, Italian, and British English.)

User Choose User to place the word in a dictionary used for a class of documents (such as documents on a specific subject or documents written by a particular person, a ''user''). You specify the name of the user dictionary in the Spelling Options dialog box.

Document Choose Document to place the word in a dictionary used only for the current document. This is handy when you are periodically checking the spelling of an evolving document and don't want the checker to stop at a correctly spelled—but unrecognized—word.

Options

Choose Options to refine the operation of the spell-checker. Set the following Spelling Options dialog box fields, as appropriate:

Always Suggest Check this box to have the spell-checker display a list of alternative words whenever it comes across a word it doesn't recognize. Turn this box off to have such a list appear only when you request it by choosing the Suggest command button.

Check Punctuation Do you want Word to let you know when it encounters punctuation that seems to be at an inappropriate location in a document?

Ignore ALL CAPS Do you want Word to skip words composed of all capital letters (such as ACLU and USA)?

Look Up Choose Complete to have Word perform an exhaustive search when seeking alternative spellings to an unrecognized word. Choose Quick to have Word assume that the first two letters of the unrecognized word are correct.

User Dictionary Choose an existing user dictionary from the text/drop-down list combo box (use the Directories list box to check other directories, if necessary) or type the name of a user dictionary you want to create. Word will check unrecognized words against this dictionary.

Undo
Choose Undo to undo the last change you made.

Remember Correction
If you press this command button, Word will remember and correct the spelling indefinitely, even with other documents and on other days. This means that if you habitually mistype *the* as *teh*, for example, Word will make the correction whenever you use Utilities Spelling. Word remembers such corrections until you delete or edit the REMEM-AM.COR file (REMEM-*XX*.COR for foreign versions) from the Word program directory (or from the local Word directory on a workstation).

Close
Choose Close to leave the spell-checker and return to your document.

Spreadsheet linking

See: Linking spreadsheets.

Starting Word

To start Word, type *word* at the DOS or OS/2 prompt. You can also be more specific about how Word starts.

If you type	Word starts
word followed by a document name	and loads the document immediately.
word/l	and loads the last document you were working on and the last glossary file.
word/y	in the scroll mode used prior to Word 5.0. (When you type at the bottom of the screen, Word scrolls up one-half screen.)
word/z	in the default switch settings used by Word 5.5.
word/k	and treats an enhanced keyboard as if it isn't enhanced (solves keyboard problems for some computers).
word/m followed immediately by the name of a macro	and runs the macro immediately. Be sure to put a space between the /m and the name of the macro, and be sure the macro is contained in the NORMAL.GLY glossary file.
word/x	and does not use expanded memory, even if it is available.
word/b*nnnn*	and sets aside for disk buffering as much conventional and expanded memory as you specify with the numbers *nnnn*. The maximum for *nnnn* is 1500, corresponding to 750 KB (because memory is measured in 512-byte units).
word/n	and operates correctly with a Novell network. (Word remembers the /n option, so you need type it only once.)

Once you start Word, you can begin typing immediately. You needn't name a document to create it; you can name a document when you save it the first time.

Storing a document

See: Saving a document.

Strikethrough characters

See: Character formatting.

Style bar

To turn on the style bar, choose View Preferences (Alt+VE) and turn on the Style Bar check box in the Preferences dialog box.

The style bar is a two-character-wide vertical column just inside a text window's left border and just to the left of the selection bar. It serves as a display area for header and footer symbols and for the key codes of paragraph and section styles.

Header and Footer Symbols

The header/footer symbols consist of one or two lowercase letters. They indicate where in the document the adjacent header or footer will print.

Symbol	Header/footer location
t	top of both even-numbered and odd-numbered pages
te	top of even-numbered pages
to	top of odd-numbered pages
tf	top of the first page only
b	bottom of both even-numbered and odd-numbered pages
be	bottom of even-numbered pages
bo	bottom of odd-numbered pages
bf	bottom of the first page only

Key Codes

Key codes consist of one or two uppercase letters, numbers, or other characters. A key code identifies the paragraph style of the adjacent paragraph or the section style of the adjacent section mark. For example, SP might be the key code for a Paragraph Normal style, and SN might be the key code for a Section Normal section style.

An asterisk in the style bar indicates that the adjacent paragraph is formatted with a style that isn't in the style sheet. A blank style bar indicates that the paragraph isn't formatted with a style or that the style has no key code.

See also: Headers and footers; Selection bar; Styles.

Styles

A style is a collection of formatting elements that you can apply to part or all of a document. A style sheet is made up of one or more styles.

A style has two components: its name and its formatting. When you record a style with Format Record Style (Alt+TR), the formatting pre-exists in the document. You copy this formatting to the style and give the style a name, which has four parts: a key code, a type, an I.D., and a remark. On the other hand, when you create a style from scratch in the style sheet window, first you create the style's name (with Insert New Style) and then you decide the style's formatting (with the commands on the Format menu).

Regardless of how you create a style, it's used in the same way. First be sure that the style you want is included in a style sheet attached to the document. Then select (highlight) the text to which you want the style to apply, press Ctrl+Y, and type the style's one-character or two-character key code. In a sense, styles and their key codes are a much more flexible version of Word's built-in formats.

In the case of dedicated styles, which are those devoted to
formatting specific elements such as standard paragraphs
or footnote reference marks, Word applies the style to the
text for you. (If you want different formatting, you can
change it by deliberately applying a different style or using
a Format command.)

Word has three major types of styles, and these types in
turn have many variations. Each major type—Character,
Paragraph, and Section—is called a "type" because it describes what it's used to format. Each variation is called a
"Style I.D."

Character Styles

Character styles control character formatting. One style
sheet can contain up to 29 character styles. Of these 29
style I.D.s, 6 are automatic styles: Page Number, Line
Number, Footnote Ref, Annotation Ref, Line Draw, and
Summary Info.

The remaining character styles, with I.D.s 1 through 23,
can be used for any character-formatting purpose.

Paragraph Styles

Paragraph styles control both the paragraph formatting and
the default character formatting of paragraphs. One style
sheet can contain up to 74 paragraph styles. Of these 74
I.D.s, 19 are automatic styles: Normal, Header/Footer,
Footnote, Annotation, Heading level 1 through Heading
level 7, Index level 1 through Index level 4, and Table level
1 through Table level 4. The remaining paragraph styles,
with I.D.s 1 through 55, can be used for any paragraph-
formatting purpose.

You can override the character-formatting component of a
paragraph style by selecting the text of a paragraph and applying a character style.

Section Styles

Section styles control the page-layout formatting of documents or sections of documents. One style sheet can contain up to 22 section styles. One of these I.D.s is an automatic style, called Normal Section. It formats a document's

page layout unless some other section formatting is
deliberately applied. The remaining section styles, with
I.D.s 1 through 21, can be used for any section-formatting
purpose.

See also: Applying a style; Automatic styles; Footnotes;
Key codes; Outlining; Recording a style; Replacing formats and styles; Searching for formats and styles; Style
bar; Style sheets; Style sheet window.

Style sheets

A style sheet is composed of styles, each of which is a combination of formatting characteristics that you apply to text.
To attach a style sheet to a document, first choose Format
Attach Style Sheet (Alt+TA). Then type the name of the
style sheet and press Enter, or choose one from the Styles
list box, and press Enter. You also can navigate through
directories, using the technique described under "Directories and subdirectories." Now you can apply a style to part
or all of a document by selecting the appropriate text and
then pressing Ctrl+Y and typing the style's one-character
or two-character key code. To examine the style sheet,
choose Format Define Styles (Alt+TD) to look in the style
sheet window.

Style sheets are powerful formatting tools because you can
change the look of an existing document simply by changing the formatting of its style sheet. In fact, when you
change a style sheet, you instantly change the appearance
of every document formatted with it.

You can further extend the power of style sheets by using a
style sheet system: two or more style sheets containing
styles that are devoted to similar formatting tasks and
have the same key codes (for example, FULL.STY and
SEMI.STY, which come with Word). After you use one
style sheet in the system to format a document, you can
change the document's appearance instantaneously by attaching another style sheet in the system.

See also: Applying a style; Attaching a style sheet; Character formatting; Detaching a style sheet; Directories and subdirectories; End mark; Filenames and extensions; Indexing; NORMAL.STY; Paragraph formatting; Ribbon; Ruler; Section formatting; Style bar; Styles; Style sheet window; Tables of contents; Tabs.

Style sheet window

Note: *In earlier versions of Word, the style sheet window was referred to as the Gallery.*

To examine, modify, create, or save a style sheet associated with the active document, choose Format Define Styles (Alt+TD) to enter the style sheet window. To leave the style sheet window and return to your document, either press Ctrl+F6 to move from window to window, or choose File Close or Window Close to close the style sheet window.

If you don't use style sheets, you need never enter the style sheet window. If you use style sheets supplied on disk in ready-to-use form, you need enter the style sheet window only to review what styles are available. To scroll through a style sheet, press PgUp or PgDn. One style at a time is selected (highlighted); press F8 to extend the selection.

The most intuitive way to create a style sheet is a style at a time, using Format Record Style (Alt+TR). This command lets you record the formatting of existing elements in a document. The English-language formatting description of each recording is called a "style." Sets of compatible styles form a style sheet. Any style can be applied to elements of documents, making even complex formatting a simple affair. If you record styles, you might enter the style sheet window only to review the descriptions or to save the styles as a style sheet.

To save a style sheet, enter the style sheet window, choose File Save As (Alt+FA), type the name of the style sheet (it can be a maximum of eight letters), and press Enter. This command functions much like its counterpart on the document window's menu bar. In the style sheet window, however, only one choice (Word) is available in the Format list box, and Word saves the file with the extension .STY instead of .DOC.

Most other commands available in the document window are also available in the style sheet window, and most function in basically the same way except that they affect styles rather than text. In addition, there are three commands (Edit Rename Style, Insert New Style, and Insert Style Sheet) that are available only in the style sheet window.

File Menu Commands

This menu contains all commands available on the document window's File menu, with the exception of Print Merge. The commands affect style sheet files—use Open to open another style sheet, Print to print the active style sheet, and so on.

Edit Menu Commands

Undo and Repeat function exactly as they do in the document window. Cut, Copy, and Paste can be used to delete, copy, and move styles, but cannot be used to manipulate text. For example, if you have text in the scrap when you open the style sheet window and you choose Paste (Alt+EP), you will receive the following message: *Text cannot be inserted into a style sheet.*

Go To and Glossary are not available in the style sheet window.

Rename Style This command is available only in the style sheet window. When you choose it (by pressing Alt+EN), you are taken to a dialog box which displays a description of the active style. To assign or change a key code, type one or two letters in the Key Code text box. To change the style I.D., make another selection from the Style I.D. drop-down list box. To add a remark, type it in the Remark text box. The style type cannot be changed.

View Menu Commands

This is a truncated version of the document window's View menu. Ribbon, Ruler, Status Bar, and Preferences work exactly as they do in the document window. Outline, Layout, and Footnotes/Annotations are not relevant in the style sheet window and thus are not included in the menu.

Insert Menu Commands

The style sheet window's Insert menu lists only two commands:

New Style Use this command to add styles to your style sheet. When you make a choice (Paragraph, Character or Section) in the Style Type drop-down list box, the Style I.D.s associated with that type are listed in the Style I.D. list box. Style I.D.s that have already been used in the style sheet, and are thus unavailable, are followed by their key code in parentheses. Select an available style I.D. in the list box or type one into the Style I.D. text box. Type in a key code and a remark, if you want, and press Enter. The style will be inserted into your document, and you can use commands from the style sheet window's Format menu to specify the formatting for the style.

Style Sheet Use this command to merge two style sheets. When you choose the command (by pressing Alt+IS), you are taken to a dialog box. In the Style Sheet Name text box, type the name of the style sheet you want to merge or choose one from the Files list box. If necessary, use the Directories list box to locate style sheet files in other directories. Then press Enter.

Format Menu Commands

Use the commands on the Format menu to specify the formatting to be associated with each style.

Character Defines the font (typeface), the size, and such other character attributes as underlining and italicizing. You can use the Character command on paragraph styles as well as on character styles because paragraph styles include default character formatting. (*See:* Character formatting.)

Paragraph Defines the paragraph (line) formatting associated with a paragraph style. For example, it controls whether lines are centered or indented. (*See:* Paragraph formatting.)

Section Determines the layout of pages: the number of columns, whether footnotes print at the bottoms of pages, and how the transition from one section to another is accomplished. It also determines whether line numbers are printed in the left page margin. (*See:* Section formatting.)

Margins Determines page size and margins. (*See:* Section formatting.)

Tabs Defines tab stops in a paragraph style. (*See:* Tabs.)

Borders Formats a paragraph style to supply a border around paragraphs formatted with the style. The border can be either a box or disconnected lines on some or all sides of the paragraph. (*See:* Lines.)

Position Formats a paragraph style to fix a paragraph to a specific place on a page. (*See:* Absolute positioning.)

Header/Footer Defines positioning for paragraph styles that apply to headers or footers. (*See:* Headers and footers.)

Utilities Menu Commands
The only Utilities menu command available in the style sheet window is Customize. (*See:* Utilities Customize.)

Macro Menu Commands
Identical to the document window's Macro menu commands. (*See:* Glossary; Macros.)

Window Menu Commands
Identical to the document window's Window menu commands. (*See:* Windows.)

Help Menu Commands
Identical to the document window's Help menu commands. (*See:* Help.)

See also: Applying a style; Automatic styles; Key codes; Proposed response; Recording a style.

Subdirectories

See: Directories and subdirectories.

Subscripts

See: Character formatting.

Summary information

To record information about a document so that you can
search for it later with the File menu's File Management
(Search) command, turn on the Prompt for Summary Info
check box in the Utilities menu's Customize dialog box.
The first time you save a document, Word presents a summary sheet for you to fill out. Provide information in as
many of the following fields as you like:

Title Do you want to give the document a descriptive title?
Type as many as 40 characters. The File Management
(Search) command doesn't search this field.

Author Who is the author of the document? Type as many
as 40 characters.

Operator Who typed or worked on the document? Type as
many as 40 characters.

Keywords Do you want to provide an additional name,
topic, or phrase that describes the document? Type as many
as 80 characters.

Comments Do you want to provide further information or
comments on the document? Type as many as 220

characters. The File Management (Search) command doesn't search this field.

Version Number What version of the document is it? Type as many as 10 characters. The File Management (Search) command doesn't search this field.

Date Created When was the document created? (Word fills this in, but you can change the information.)

Date Saved When was the document last saved? (Word fills this in, but you can change the information.)

After filling in some, all, or none of these fields, press Enter to save the document. To update the summary information, use the Search command in the File Management dialog box to find the document and the Summary command in the dialog box to revise the contents of the summary information.

Summary sheets are formatted to print in the font specified in the Character Summary Info dedicated style, if a style sheet is in use and if the style has been defined.

See also: Automatic styles; File management; Saving a document.

Superscripts and subscripts

See: Character formatting.

Synonyms

See: Thesaurus.

Tables of contents

Creating a table of contents based on the headings in a
document is a two-step process. The first step is to format
the headings; the second step is to compile the table of
contents.

Formatting the Headings

You can format headings in three ways:

Heading styles If you're using a style sheet, format headings with the dedicated paragraph styles Heading 1 through
Heading 4. (Although you can assign seven Heading level
styles, your table of contents will include a maximum of
four levels.)

Promotion and demotion If you're not using a style sheet,
hold down Shift and press F2 to enter outline view, highlight any paragraph that is to be a heading, and then hold
down Ctrl and press 9. Now, to adjust the level of the heading, hold down Ctrl and press 9 (to promote the heading to
a higher level) or hold down Alt and press 0 (to demote the
heading to a lower level).

Coding with hidden text At the beginning of each heading, hold down Ctrl and press H (AH if a macro uses
Ctrl+H) to turn on hidden text. Then type .C.—followed by
colons if you want a level 2 or lower heading. For example,
for a level 2 heading, first turn on hidden text and then type
.C.: For a level 3 heading, type .C.:: If you want only part
of the heading to be listed in the table of contents, use a
semicolon, formatted in hidden text, to mark the end of the
entry. (If the heading itself contains a colon or a semicolon,
enclose the entire entry except the coding in quotation
marks. You can format the quotation marks as hidden so
that they won't print.)

Compiling the Table of Contents

To compile the table of contents, choose Insert Table of
Contents (Alt+IC), set the following dialog box fields as
appropriate, and press Enter.

Create Table of Contents from Choose Outline to compile a table of contents based on the document's headings as they appear in outline view. The only headings omitted are those that are collapsed from view when outline view is turned on. Choose Codes to compile a table of contents based on hidden-text codes. The default code is C. Unless you change it, the Table of Contents command searches the document for table entries that start with .C. or .c. (hidden text). You can use any letter except D, G, I, L, or P.

Show Page Numbers Do you want to include page numbers in your table of contents?

Separate by If you turned on the Show Page Numbers check box, what separator do you want between the page numbers and the text of the table? The default is ^t, representing a tab character. Unless you change it, the ^t causes the Table of Contents command to place a tab character between each table entry and its page number. It also places a right-aligned tab stop into the table's paragraph formatting so that page numbers print on the right side of the page.

Indent each level The default is 0.4". Unless you change it or choose the Use Style Sheet option, Word indents each subentry 0.4" relative to the higher-level entry preceding it. Choose Use Style Sheet to use the automatic Table level styles in a style sheet to individually control the formatting of each level of entry. Word formats the table of contents according to the Table level 1, Table level 2, Table level 3, and Table level 4 styles in the style sheet. If some of these styles aren't in the style sheet or if no style sheet is attached, Word uses standard paragraph formatting for the entries.

See also: Hidden text; Indexing; Outlining; Styles.

Tabs

To insert a tab character in your document at the location of the cursor, press Tab. The tab character, normally invisible,

fills the space between its insertion point and the location
of the next tab stop to the right. Although a tab character
can fill many consecutive spaces, you select, delete, and
copy the tab character as you do any other single character.
To display the tab character on the screen as a small, right-
facing arrow, choose View Preferences and turn on the
Tabs check box in the Preferences dialog box.

Formatting the tab stop to the right of the tab character determines how many spaces the tab character fills and how
the text that is typed after it appears. Tab characters are
part of your document's content; tab stops are part of paragraph formatting.

Word presets tab stops evenly across every paragraph.
Preset tab stops are adequate for some simple needs: Each
time you press the tab key to insert a tab character, you
move to the next stop. The spacing is 0.5 inch unless you
change Default Tab in the Utilities menu's Customize dialog box.

You can override preset tab stops by formatting a paragraph with other tab stops. A preset tab stop vanishes when
you place another tab stop at the same location or to the
right of it.

The easiest way to set and move tab stops is with the ruler.

To manipulate tab stops with the Format menu's Tabs command, press Alt+TT to call up the Tabs dialog box. Use the
following fields to alter tab stop settings, and then press
Enter:

Position How far from the left margin (not the left edge of
the page) do you want the tab stop?

Alignment When you type data "under" a tab stop, what
part of the typed text do you want to line up with the stop?
Its left end? Center? Right end? Decimal point? (When you
choose Decimal, text without a decimal point is aligned as
if you'd chosen Right; that is, the right end of the text
"under" the tab stop is aligned with the stop.)

Vertical is a special choice because it really isn't a tab stop or form of alignment. To place a vertical line at the position of the tab stop, choose Vertical. This feature is useful when you're creating tables and you want vertical lines at specific locations.

Leader Do you want a leader character in the otherwise blank space leading to the tab stop? If not, choose None. Otherwise, choose a period (.), hyphen (-), or underline (_).

Set When you have specified a tab stop's position, alignment, and leader character (if any), choose the Set command button to establish the tab stop.

Clear To remove the tab stop that appears in the Tab Position text box, choose the Clear command button.

Clear All To remove all custom tab stops from the selected paragraph(s), choose Clear All.

To create a table that uses different tab stops in different lines, make each line of the table a separate paragraph.

See also: Lines; Mouse; Paragraph formatting; Ruler; Styles.

Text box

A text box is a type of dialog-box field that, instead of providing preset choices, allows you to type in a response. Text boxes are represented by square brackets and often contain a default choice, which can be accepted or typed over.

A text box followed by a downward-facing arrow is called a text/drop-down list combo box.

See also: Dialog box; Drop-down list box.

Text mode

See: Display mode.

Text window

You can open as many as nine text windows at once; when
you start Word, however, only one is present. Each window
can contain a different document or a different part or view
of the same document.

See also: Windows.

Thesaurus

To see a list of synonyms for a word you've just typed or
selected (highlighted), choose Utilities Thesaurus (Alt+UT
or Shift+F7). A dialog box will appear.

If the selected word appears in Word's thesaurus, the dialog box will display two list boxes. The first one, Definitions, lists basic meanings for the term. The second one,
Synonyms, lists the synonyms for the term which corre-
spond to the meaning highlighted in the Definitions box.
As you scroll through the definitions list, the synonyms list
will change.

If the selected word does not appear in the thesaurus, a
slightly different version of the dialog box appears. Instead
of Definitions and Synonyms list boxes, this dialog box displays an alphabetic list of words which *are* in the thesaurus
and which begin with the same letter or letters as your
original term.

Both versions of the Thesaurus dialog box contain three
command buttons, in addition to the Close button:

Replace Choose this command button to replace your
original term with a selected (highlighted) term from either
the Synonyms list box (if your word was in the thesaurus)
or the alphabetic list of thesaurus entries (if your word was
not in the thesaurus).

Synonyms Choose this command button to display a list of
synonyms for a selected (highlighted) term from either the
Synonyms list box (if your word was in the thesaurus) or
the alphabetic list of thesaurus entries (if your word was
not in the thesaurus).

Original If you have used the Synonyms command button
to see new lists of synonyms, choosing this command button will return you to your original synonyms list.

Type

See: Recording a style; Styles; Style sheet window.

Typefaces

See: Character formatting; Downloadable fonts; Printer
files; Ribbon.

Typesetting

See: PostScript.

Undelete

See: Undoing an edit.

Underlining

To underline characters, first select (highlight) the characters and then use one of these three methods:

Format Character

Choose Format Character (Alt+TC), turn on the Underline check box, and press Enter.

Built-in Format

Hold down Ctrl and press U. If a style sheet is attached to your document, hold down Ctrl and press AU.

Styles

If a style sheet is attached to your document and if it includes a character style for underlining, press Ctrl+Y and type the one-character or two-character key code of the style, such as UC (for Underline Character). To format a single character, press Ctrl+Y and type the key code twice. To see which styles are available in a style sheet, choose Format Apply Style (Alt+TY) and choose Character in the Style Type drop-down list box, or choose Format Define Styles (Alt+TD) to look in the style sheet window.

To underline characters as you type them, apply the format and type.

See also: Built-in formats; Character formatting; Key codes; Ribbon; Styles; Style sheet window.

Undoing an edit

To undo the last editing act, choose Edit Undo (Alt+EU or
Alt+Backspace). For example, you can use Edit Undo to
restore text you've just deleted or to change characters
you've just formatted as italic back to normal.

A new editing act begins whenever you move the cursor
without typing or deleting the content of your document or
when you choose a command or press Ins or Del.

See also: Repeating an edit or macro.

Utilities Customize

Along with View Preferences, the Utilities menu's Customize command (Alt+UU) is used to customize features that
in earlier versions of Word were controlled by the Options
command. Utilities Customize offers the following choices:

(Autosave) Frequency Do you want Word to periodically
save your work in a special backup file? If so, type a number (representing minutes) in this field. (*See:* Autosave.)

(Autosave) Confirm If you choose Yes, Word will pause
before autosaving and ask you *Do you want to back up
changes with autosave now?* This field has meaning only
if the Frequency field has a value other than 0. (*See:*
Autosave.)

Background Pagination Check this box to have Word continuously calculate the location of page breaks and place
the current page number in the screen's lower left corner,
on the status bar. Turn off the check box to have Word update page breaks only when you print a document (with
File Print), preview a document (with File Print Preview),
create an index or table (with Insert Index or Insert

Table of Contents), or deliberately repaginate a document (with Utilities Repaginate Now).

Prompt for Summary Info Do you want Word to present you with a blank summary sheet the first time you save a document? (*See:* File management.)

Widow/Orphan Control Do you want to prevent Word from printing one line of a multiline paragraph at the top or bottom of a page? If you do not check this box, Word always prints as many lines on a page as are allowed by the page's formatting.

Use Word 5.0 Function Keys Do you want to use Word 5.5's function-key assignments or Word 5.0's? If you check this box, Word 5.5 will emulate the function-key mapping used by Word 5.0 (except for the F1 key, which is permanently assigned to Help).

Use INS for Overtype Key Do you want the Insert key to toggle overtype mode (the default Word 5.5 setting) or to insert text from the scrap (its function in Word 5.0)? The setting of this option also affects the functions of the Delete key. (*See:* Appendix.)

Show Keys on Menus Do you want Word to display the shortcut key for a command (for example, Alt+Backspace for the Edit menu's Undo command) next to that command's name on the drop-down menu?

Decimal Do you want the decimal character to be a period (decimal point) or a comma?

Date When using the *date* and *dateprint* glossary entries, do you want the date to follow the month-day-year format (MDY) or the day-month-year format (DMY)?

Time Do you want Word to use a 12-hour clock (4:15 A.M., 4:15 P.M.) or a 24-hour clock (4:15, 16:15)?

Measure Which of five units of measure do you want Word to use to express distances and measurements in various Format command fields? The default choice in the United States is inches (In), and the instructions in this book assume inches.

Mute Do you want to turn off Word's audible alarm, which sounds when you attempt something impossible?

Line Draw Character When you use the Line Draw command, which of 12 characters do you want Word to use to draw lines? Hold down the Alt key and press the Down direction key to see a scrollable list of suggested characters, or type the desired character. What is printed depends on the character you choose in this field, on how the character is formatted (including its font), and on the capabilities of your printer. (*See:* Automatic styles; Lines.)

Default Tab When a paragraph isn't formatted with explicit tab stops, how far apart do you want Word's default tab stops to be placed? Word assumes 0.5" unless you change the setting. (*See:* Tabs.)

Speller Name Specify the disk, directory, and name of the dictionary used by Word's spell-checker. This allows you to use more than one main dictionary—for multiple languages, for example. You can use the Directories list box to navigate among your directories and drives.

Preferences Choosing this button takes you to the Preferences dialog box, which is also reached by choosing Preferences from the View menu.

See also: View Preferences.

Variant

The term "variant" is not used in Windows 5.5. Variants are now known as "Style I.D.s."

See: Recording a style; Styles; Style sheet window.

View Preferences

Along with the Utilities menu's Customize command, the
View menu's Preferences command controls features that
in earlier versions of Word were controlled by the Options
command. The Preferences dialog box offers the following
choices:

Show All Do you want to display all normally invisible
(nonprintable) characters on the screen? Checking this box
automatically turns on the other check boxes in the Non-
printing Characters portion of the dialog box. This causes
all of the following to be displayed on the screen: paragraph marks (¶), newline characters (↓), optional (nonrequired) hyphens (-), hidden text, Spacebar spaces (·),
and tab characters (→). Somewhat inconsistently, turning
off this check box does *not* turn off its associated check
boxes—the boxes must be unchecked individually.

Tabs Do you want to display tab characters (→)?

Optional Hyphens Do you want to display optional
hyphens (-)?

Paragraph Marks Do you want to display paragraph
marks (¶) and newline characters (↓)?

Spaces Do you want to display spacebar spaces (·)?

Hidden Text Do you want to display hidden text? In a
graphics mode, hidden text will display with a dotted underline. In a text mode, it will display as boldfaced (on
monochrome systems) or in a different color (on color systems). If this check box is turned off but the Paragraph
Marks check box is turned on, the presence of hidden text
will be indicated by a double-headed arrow. (*See:* Hidden
text.)

(Show) Line breaks Do you want lines on the screen to
break as they will when printed? If so, turn this check box
on. Turn it off if you prefer an approximation of line layout
that might be easier to read on the screen.

(Show) Menu: Yes No Do you want the command menu at the top of the screen to be displayed during text entry?

(Show) Style Bar Do you want to activate the style bar, which shows (to the left of text) the key codes of paragraph and section styles? (*See:* Style bar.)

(Show) Window Borders Do you want to display window borders when only one window is open?

(Show) Message Bar Do you want the message bar (the bottom line of the screen) to display at all times?

(Scroll Bars) Horizontal Do you want to display the horizontal scroll bar?

(Scroll Bars) Vertical Do you want to display the vertical scroll bar?

Cursor Control How fast do you want the cursor to move when you press a direction key? Enter a number from 0 (slowest) to 9 (fastest). A setting of 2 or 3 is common.

Show Line Numbers Do you want Word to display, on the status bar next to the page number, the cursor's line number in the current page? Turning on this check box significantly slows certain Word operations.

Count Blank Space If the Show Line Numbers check box is turned on, do you want Word to count lines that are blank due to paragraph formatting? If you check this box, Word will count all lines that exist due to space-before and space-after paragraph formatting, as well as lines created due to content.

Display Mode Which display mode do you want to use? Hold down the Alt key and press the Down direction key to see a list of the graphics and text display modes available for your display adapter and monitor. (*See:* Display mode.)

Colors Choose this command button to go to a dialog box that allows you to choose colors for elements on the screen. (*See:* Colors on the screen.)

Customize Choose this command button to go to the Customize dialog box, which is also reached by choosing Customize from the Utilities menu.

See also: Utilities Customize.

Wildcards

Use the wildcard characters *?* and *** to broaden or narrow choices Word offers in Files list boxes or when you search with Edit Search, Edit Replace, or with the File Management (Search) command. The wildcard character *?* represents any single character. The *** represents any series of characters.

For example, if you choose File Open (by pressing Alt+FO or Alt+Ctrl+F2), the Files list box shows a list of all files ending in the extension .DOC. If you type **.** in the File Name text box and then press Enter, the screen shows a list of all files. If you type *art.** and then press Enter, the screen shows all files with the name *art*; for example, ART.DOC and ART.BAK. If you type **.bak* and then press Enter, the screen shows all files that have .BAK as their extension.

You can also use wildcards in the Printer File field of File Printer Setup and then press Enter to see a subset of the available printer files. To see a list of printer files for Hewlett-Packard printers, for example, type *HP** and press Enter.

Wildcards are permitted in the Text to Search for fields of Edit Search and Edit Replace and in the Search Paths, Author, Operator, Keywords, and Text fields of the File Management (Search) command.

See also: File management; Opening a document; Printer files; Replacing text; Searching for text.

Window borders

To turn off window borders, choose View Preferences (Alt+VE), turn off the Window Borders check box, and press Enter.

When more than one window is displayed on the screen, Word keeps all borders on.

Windows

You can open as many as nine windows at once; each can hold a different document or different views of a document.

You can use the following commands from the Window menu to control and manipulate windows. However, using a mouse is more efficient. (*See:* Mouse.)

New Window

To open a copy of the current document in an additional window, choose New Window (Alt+WN).

Arrange All

Choose this command (by pressing Alt+WA) to arrange your open windows so that they all display on the screen at once, without overlapping.

Maximize

Windows share space on the screen unless you use this command (by pressing Alt+WX or Ctrl+F10) to "maximize" your windows. When windows are maximized, each uses the whole screen, and only one window is displayed at a time. To move from window to window, whether windows are maximized or not, press Ctrl+F6. (If you write macros that use more than one window, don't overlook the power of the reserved variable *Maximized*, described in the Macros discussion.)

Restore

If you have used Window Maximize to maximize your windows, use this command to return them to their original sizes. Press Alt+WR or Ctrl+F5.

Move

To move the active window, choose Window Move (Alt+WM
or Ctrl+F7). Use the direction keys to reposition the window, and then press Enter.

Size

To change the size of the active window, choose Window
Size (Alt+WS or Ctrl+F8). Use the direction keys to resize
the window, and then press Enter.

Split

To split a window into two panes, choose Window Split
(Alt+WT). The split (a double horizontal line) will appear
at the top of the window; use the direction keys to move it
down to the desired position, and then press Enter.

Using a window split allows you to keep a certain part of
your document visible in one pane while you scroll or edit
in the other.

To close the window split, choose Window Split again.
This time, use the direction keys to move the split line to
the very top or the very bottom of the window, and then
press Enter.

Close

If you have one document that is open in more than one
window, you can use Window Close (Alt+WC or Ctrl+F4)
to close one or more of the windows.

If the document is open only in a single window, choosing
Window Close is equivalent to choosing File Close. If you
have made editing changes since the last time you saved
the document, Word will ask *Do you want to save changes
to (filename)?*

(Document Names)

This command does not really have a name: It consists of
the numbered list of open windows which appears at the
bottom of the Window drop-down menu.

The active window is listed with a dot to its left. To change
the active window, press Alt+W (to call up the Window

menu) and then press the number of the desired window. When the Help window is open, it always appears last on the list and, instead of a number, is labeled with the letter H.

Keyboard

Actions possible with the keyboard fall into several categories: entering and editing both printable characters and spacing characters such as paragraph marks; using commands (both general procedures and specific techniques); formatting; and operating in special modes such as outline view and layout view.

The following pages list the keyboard possibilities for Word 5.5. Earlier versions of Word, including 5.0, use key combinations that often are quite different.

Function keys

The function keys for Word 5.5 have been assigned functions similar to Windows applications and are different from previous versions of Word.

Word 5.5 vs. 5.0 emulation When the Use 5.0 Function Keys field of the Utilities menu's Customize dialog box has been checked, the function keys perform more or less like Word 5.0 function keys. The major exception is the F1 key: F1 is permanently assigned to Help in Word 5.5. So if you're using the 5.0 version of the function keys, you must use the Alt+Shift+F1 key combination to move to the next window (the function of F1 in Word 5.0).

Key	Word 5.5 function	Word 5.0 emulation
F1	Request on-screen help	Request on-screen help
Shift+F1	Unassigned, but used by MasterWord as "Extra Help."	Undo last edit (Edit Undo)
Ctrl+F1	Unassigned, but used by MasterWord as "Action Help."	Toggle between Maximize and Restore (zooming)
Alt+F1	Move cursor to next field (first character after next right chevron: »)	Move to ruler to set tab stops
Alt+Shift+F1	Move cursor to previous field (first character after previous right chevron: »)	Move to next window
F2	Calculate a highlighted expression	Calculate a highlighted expression
Shift+F2	Turn outline mode on or off (View Outline)	Turn outline mode on or off (View Outline)
Ctrl+F2	Choose formatting for characters (Format Character)	Turn paragraph into header (Format Header/Footer)
Alt+F2	Name and save current file (File Save As)	Turn paragraph into footer (Format Header/Footer)
Alt+Ctrl+F2	Open existing file (File Open)	Open existing file (File Open)
Alt+Shift+F2	Save active file (File Save As)	Unassigned
Alt+Shift+Ctrl+F2	Print active file (File Print)	Print active file (File Print)
F3	Expand previous or selected glossary term	Expand previous or selected glossary term

Key	Word 5.5 function	Word 5.0 emulation
Shift+F3	Toggle case of selected text	Record macro (Macro Record)
Ctrl+F3	Record macro (Macro Record)	Toggle macro step mode
Alt+F3	Copy selected text to scrap (Edit Copy)	Copy selected text to scrap (Edit Copy)
F4	Repeat last edit or macro (Edit Repeat)	Repeat last edit (Edit Repeat)
Shift+F4	Repeat last search	Repeat last search
Ctrl+F4	Close active window (Window Close)	Toggle case of selected text
Alt+F4	Exit Word and return to DOS or OS/2 prompt (File Exit Word)	Toggle layout view (View Layout)
F5	Jump to specified location (Edit Go To)	Toggle overtype mode
Shift+F5	Once in outline view, toggle between its edit and organize modes	Once in outline view, toggle between its edit and organize modes
Ctrl+F5	Restore document window to un-maximized state (Window Restore)	Toggle linedraw mode
Alt+F5	Toggle overtype mode	Go to specified location (Edit Go To)
Shift+Ctrl+F5	Insert a bookmark (Insert Bookmark)	Insert a bookmark (Insert Bookmark)
F6	Move to next pane in active window	Turn on extend-selection mode
Shift+F6	Move to previous pane in active window	Toggle column selection

Key	Word 5.5 function	Word 5.0 emulation
Ctrl+F6	Move to next window	Use thesaurus (Utilities Thesaurus)
Alt+F6	Select word in which cursor appears, or if it is already selected, select next word	Check spelling (Utilities Spelling)
Shift+Ctrl+F6	Move to previous window	Move to previous window
F7	Use spell-checker (Utilities Spelling)	Select previous word
Shift+F7	Use thesaurus (Utilities Thesaurus)	Select previous sentence
Ctrl+F7	Move active window (Window Move)	Open existing file (File Open)
Alt+F7	Toggle Show Line breaks (View Preferences)	Toggle Show Line breaks
F8	Turn on extend-selection mode and select character, word, sentence, paragraph, or entire document (depending on how many times you press it)	Select next word
Shift+F8	Shrink selection (if F8 key has been pressed more than once)	Select next sentence
Ctrl+F8	Adjust size of active window (Window Size; press Enter when done)	Print active file (File Print)

Key	Word 5.5 function	Word 5.0 emulation
Alt+F8	Select sentence in which cursor appears, or if it is already selected, select next sentence	Choose character formatting (Format Character)
Shift+Ctrl+F8	Turn column-selection mode on or off	Turn column-selection mode on or off
F9	Update links to other files (established with Insert File)	Select previous paragraph
Shift+F9	Print active document (File Print)	Select line that contains cursor
Ctrl+F9	Preview how document looks when printed (File Print Preview)	Preview how document looks when printed (Print Preview)
Alt+F9	Toggle between last two display modes	Toggle between last two display modes
F10	Activate menu bar	Select next paragraph
Shift+F10	Select entire document	Select entire document
Ctrl+F10	Maximize (zoom) all windows (Window Maximize)	Save current file (File Save)
Alt+F10	Select paragraph in which cursor appears, or if it is already selected, select next paragraph	Record formatting as a style (Format Record Style)
Shift+Ctrl+F10	Activate ruler	Move cursor to ruler

Key	Word 5.5 function	Word 5.0 emulation
F11	Move cursor to next field (first character after next right chevron: »)	Collapse current heading (in outline view)
Shift+F11	Move cursor to previous field (first character after previous right chevron: »)	Collapse body text (in outline view)
F12	Name and save active file (File Save As)	Expand current heading (in outline view)
Shift+F12	Save active file (File Save As)	Expand body text (in outline view)
Ctrl+F12	Open existing file (File Open)	Expand all text and headings (in outline view)
Shift+Ctrl+F12	Print active file (File Print)	Print active file (File Print)

Turning modes on and off

Word operates in a variety of "modes." Although only certain of these are called modes by Microsoft, all of the following key combinations cause Word to shift its method of operation in a significant way.

To turn this mode on or off:	Press:
Extend Selection (turn it on)	F8
Extend Selection (turn it off)	Esc
Column Selection	Ctrl+Shift+F8
Numeric Lock	Num Lock
Scroll Lock	Scroll Lock
Uppercase letters	Caps Lock

To turn this mode on or off:	Press:
Overtype	Alt+F5 (Ins key also works if Use INS for Overtype Key check box is checked in Utilities Customize dialog box.)
Macro Record	Ctrl+F3
Step Macro	Alt+MR, then Alt+S (in dialog box), then Enter
Line Draw (on/off)	Alt+UL/Esc
Show Line Breaks	Alt+F7
Previous video mode	Alt+F9
Print Preview (on/off)	Ctrl+F9/Esc
Outline View	Shift+F2

Entering and editing text

Copying, Deleting, and Inserting Text

To:	Press:
Insert (paste) text stored in glossary	F3
Copy selected text to scrap	Ctrl+Ins (or Alt+F3)
Delete character to left of cursor	Backspace
Delete word to left of cursor	Ctrl+Backspace

The functions of the Insert and Delete keys in Word 5.5 can change depending on the status of the Use INS for Overtype Key field in the Utilities menu's Customize dialog box. If the field is checked (if it is turned on), follow the instructions in the second column of the table. If it is not checked (if it is turned off), follow the instructions in the third column.

To:	INS for Overtype Key on:	INS for Overtype Key off:
Permanently delete (kill) selected text	Del	Shift+Del
Delete (cut) selected text to scrap	Shift+Del	Del
Insert (paste) text from scrap	Shift+Ins	Ins

Spacing Characters

To insert:	Press:
Normal space	Spacebar
Nonbreaking space (keeps both words on same line)	Shift+Ctrl+Spacebar
Tab character	Tab
Paragraph mark	Enter
New-line character (forces new line, same paragraph)	Shift+Enter
New-column character (forces new column)	Alt+IB; choose Column; press Enter
New-page character (forces new page)	Alt+IB; choose Page; press Enter, or Ctrl+Enter
New-section character (forces new section)	Alt+IB; choose Section; press Enter
Optional hyphen (appears only when word breaks at end of line)	Ctrl+Hyphen (on top row of keyboard)
Nonbreaking hyphen (keeps both words on same line)	Shift+Ctrl+Hyphen (on top row of keyboard)

Printable Characters

To type a:	Press:
Number	Numbers on top row or, if Num Lock key is on, keypad
Symbol such as $, %, or @	Shift and simultaneously press key showing symbol (Caps Lock key won't work)

To type a:	Press:
Nonbreaking hyphen (keeps both words on same line)	Shift+Ctrl+Hyphen (on top row of keyboard)
Optional hyphen (appears only when word breaks at end of line)	Ctrl+Hyphen (on top row of keyboard)
Dash	Alt+Ctrl+Hyphen (on top row of keyboard); twice in a row
Foreign, mathematical, or graphics character	Turn on Num Lock, then hold Alt key and type character's number code on keypad

Using menus and dialog boxes

Press Alt or F10 to activate the menu bar. Press the emphasized character (usually it's bold) of the command family menu you desire. This is the *accelerator key* for the menu, and happens to be the first letter of each command family name, except for Format, where it is ''t.'' Then press the emphasized character of the command in the drop-down menu. You can also use the direction keys to move around in the menu bar. Press Esc to deactivate the menus.

To undo a command, press Alt+Backspace or choose Edit Undo (Alt+EU).

Many commands produce dialog boxes. Use the following keystrokes to adjust the settings in the dialog boxes:

To:	Press:
Move to next option	Tab
Move to previous option	Shift+Tab
Move to specific option	Alt+Emphasized letter of option

To:	Press:
View options on drop-down list (in fields with down-facing arrows after them)	F4 or Alt+Down direction key
Select item in list box	Direction keys
Toggle check boxes on and off	Spacebar (or Alt+Emphasized letter of field)
Select options in option box	Direction keys
Execute command when all options are set	Enter
Cancel dialog box and lose any option changes made	Esc

Formatting

Using the Ribbon

To:	Do this:
Turn ribbon on and off	Alt+VB (View Ribbon)
Move cursor to Style field	Ctrl+AS
Move cursor to Font field	Ctrl+AF
Move to Points field	Ctrl+AP
Apply style, font, or point size listed on ribbon	With text selected, use direction keys to scroll to desired option in list box; press Enter
Leave ribbon without making changes	Esc

Using the Ruler

To:	Press:
Turn ruler on and off	Alt+VR (View Ruler)
Move cursor to ruler (and turn it on if it is not on already)	Shift+Ctrl+F10

To:	**Press:**
Return cursor to document and save changes made in ruler	Enter
Return cursor to document without making changes with ruler	Esc

Adjusting custom tab stops with the ruler There are five types of tab stops, each represented on the ruler by a different character:

L	Left alignment
R	Right alignment
C	Center alignment
|	Vertical alignment
D	Decimal alignment
To insert custom tab stops	Use direction keys to position cursor; press first letter of tab type (L, C, R, D, or V)
To move custom tab stops	With cursor on tab stop, hold down Ctrl and use Left and Right direction keys to reposition tab

Three types of leader characters can be used with a tab stop:

------	Hyphen
......	Period
_____	Underscore
To add leader characters to tab stops	With cursor on tab stop, press Period (.), Hyphen (-), or Underscore (_)
To delete custom tab stops	Move cursor to tab stop with direction keys; press Del

Three paragraph indents are shown on the ruler:

¦	First line indent
[	Left indent
]	Right indent

All three of these can be changed with the mouse. Position the mouse cursor on the indent character, press the right mouse button, reposition the character, and release the button. To reposition the indents with the keyboard, choose Format Paragraph and adjust the values in the Indent fields.

Speed Formatting with Built-In Formats

Character formats To use a speed formatting key, hold down Ctrl and press the letter of the built-in format (for example, Ctrl+B for bold). If a macro in your glossary begins with Ctrl and the letter of a built-in format, press Ctrl+A and then the built-in format code—for example, Ctrl+AB to make characters bold.

If a style sheet is attached, Ctrl+Spacebar gives the selected characters whatever formatting is specified in the character portion of the governing paragraph style.

To make characters:	Press:
Bold	Ctrl+B (Ctrl+AB if there's a macro conflict)
Italic	Ctrl+I (Ctrl+AI)
Small caps	Ctrl+K (Ctrl+AK)
Underlined	Ctrl+U (Ctrl+AU)
Double underlined	Ctrl+D (Ctrl+AD)
Superscripted	Ctrl+Shift+= (Ctrl+A+Shift+=)
Subscripted	Ctrl+= (Ctrl+A=)
Hidden	Ctrl+H (Ctrl+AH)
Standard (remove all character formats)	Ctrl+Spacebar (Ctrl+A+Spacebar)
Standard (remove character formats except font and size)	Ctrl+Z (Ctrl+AZ)

Paragraph formats To use a speed formatting key, hold down Ctrl and press the letter of the built-in format (for example, Ctrl+C for centered). If a macro in your glossary begins with Ctrl and the letter of a built-in format, press Ctrl+A and then the built-in format code—for example, Ctrl+AC to make paragraphs centered. To make it run

faster, omit the A and replace it with a doubling of the
character—in this case CC (or Ctrl+Shift+CC).

Format:	Press:
Centered	Ctrl+C (Ctrl+AC if there is a macro conflict)
Left alignment	Ctrl+L (Ctrl+AL)
Right alignment	Ctrl+R (Ctrl+AR)
Justified	Ctrl+J (Ctrl+AJ)
Increase left indent	Ctrl+N (Ctrl+AN)
Decrease left indent	Ctrl+M (Ctrl+AM)
Hanging indention (indent all lines but first)	Ctrl+T (Ctrl+AT)
Indent from left and right (for block quotations and so on)	Ctrl+Q (Ctrl+AQ)
Single line spacing	Ctrl+1 (Ctrl+A1)
Double line spacing	Ctrl+2 (Ctrl+A2)
Open paragraph spacing (blank line before paragraph)	Ctrl+O (Ctrl+AO) (the letter O)
Normal paragraph	Ctrl+X (Ctrl+AX)

Operating in special modes

Outline View

The purposes of several keys change when you move from
normal document view to outline view. Outline view has
two modes: Outline Edit and Outline Organize.

To:	Press:
Move between document view and outline view	Shift+F2 or Alt+VO
Toggle between outline edit and outline organize	Shift+F5
Lower heading one level	Ctrl+0 (zero)
Raise heading one level	Ctrl+9
Add body text to outline	Ctrl+X; type text

To:	Press:
Collapse subheadings and body text	Minus (on number pad) or Ctrl+8
Collapse body text below heading	Shift+Minus (on number pad) or Ctrl+Shift+8
Expand next heading level and body text	Plus (on number pad) or Ctrl+7
Expand body text below heading	Shift+Plus (on number pad)
Expand all headings to specified level	Alt+Shift; type desired heading level (use numbers on top of keyboard)
Expand all headings	Select entire outline (Shift+5); press * (on number pad)
Expand all body text	Select entire outline; press Shift+Plus (on number pad) or Shift+Ctrl+7

Outline organize mode only When you are in organize mode, the word ORGANIZE appears on the status line.

To:	Press:
Select previous heading of same level as current heading	Up direction key
Select next heading of same level as current heading	Down direction key
Select previous heading of any level	Left direction key
Select next heading of any level	Right direction key
Select nearest heading at next higher level	Home
Select last subheading at next lower level	End
Extend selection to subsequent headings of same level	F8+Down direction key

Layout View

To enter layout view, choose View Layout (Alt+VL). The
characters *LY* will appear on the status line.

To move to:	Press:
Beginning of previous paragraph	Ctrl+Up
Next column or element (to right)	Alt+5(keypad)+Right (Num Lock off)
Previous column or element (to left)	Alt+5(keypad)+Left (Num Lock off)

When Working with a Form

To move to:	Press:
Next field (indicated by »)	Alt+F1
Previous field (indicated by »)	Alt+Shift+F1

Keys for Microsoft Windows

If you run Microsoft Word as a non-Windows application
under Microsoft Windows 3.0, certain key combinations let
you move between Word and the Windows environment.

To:	Press:
Switch to next application (program) or minimized icon	Alt+Esc
Switch to next application, restoring applications that are running as icons	Alt+Tab
Switch to Windows Task List to choose among all programs currently running	Ctrl+Esc
Copy screen to Windows clipboard	Print Screen
Switch Word to windowed application (386 Enhanced mode only)	Alt+Enter

Peter Rinearson

Journalist Peter Rinearson has been using word processors since 1976. He has received several national writing awards, including a Pulitzer Prize for an account of the creation of the Boeing 757 jetliner, published in the *Seattle Times*. He is the creator of MasterWord, a companion disk to Microsoft® Word 5.5, and has written two other books for Microsoft Press: *Microsoft® Word Style Sheets* (with JoAnne Woodcock), and the forthcoming *Running Microsoft Word 5.5*.

The manuscript for this book was prepared and submitted to Microsoft Press in electronic form. Text files were processed and formatted using Microsoft Word.

Principal word processors: Debbie Kem and Judith Bloch
Principal proofreader: Deborah Long
Principal typographer: Ruth Pettis
Interior text designer: Darcie S. Furlan
Cover designer: Celeste Design
Cover color separator: Rainier Color Corp.

Text composition by Microsoft Press in Times Roman with display in Futura Heavy, using the Magna composition system and the Linotronic 300 laser imagesetter.

Printed on recycled paper stock.